The Beginnings of Social Understanding

The Beginnings of
Social Understanding

Judy Dunn

Harvard University Press
Cambridge, Massachusetts
1988

This book is printed on acid-free paper, and its binding materials
have been chosen for strength and durability.

Library of Congress Cataloging-in-Publication Data
Dunn, Judy
  The beginnings of social understanding.
  Bibliography: p.
  Includes index.
  1. Social perception in children. 2. Social inter-
action in children. 3. Family. I. Title.
BF723.S6D86 1988   155.4'23   88–766
ISBN 0-674-06453-4 (alk. paper)

Preface

This book happened to grow out of quite a different enterprise. About seven years ago I was studying firstborn children over the period when a sibling was born, in order to see the developing relationship between the two young children and its connections with other family relationships. But that study, which involved long observations in the children's homes, developed in an unexpected direction. Sitting in the kitchens and living rooms of the families, watching the games, jokes, and disputes between the siblings and their complex relationships with the parents, I became fascinated with the glimpses of understanding that much of the children's social behavior appeared to reflect. Not only the firstborn children, but most surprisingly some of their younger siblings early in the second year showed a clear practical grasp of how to annoy or comfort the other child. This suggested powers of understanding in these young children well beyond those we might expect from studies of children outside the familiar emotional world of the family— but the incidents involving the younger siblings were too few to provide more than provocative anecdotes. I decided to pursue the issue with systematic studies of children's understanding of the feelings and behavior of others in their family world, observing the children within the drama and excitement of family life, and this led to the research on which my book is based.

I must emphasize that these *are* systematic studies. Although I have used quotations and examples to illustrate the children's growing understanding, they are not simply anecdotes—bizarre or freakish incidents at odds with the general pattern found for the fifty-two secondborn children we studied, after the eighty children of the initial research. Rather the examples serve to support conclusions drawn from careful, documented study. Thus the instances of children's teasing, justifications, and excuses, their behavior as witnesses to disputes between others, their cooperative behavior and response to distress in others, their questions and narratives about others, all illustrate actions for which I also give frequencies for the full sample of the relevant study (frequencies are indicated in the figures and appendix tables). A partial exception is the material on jokes. Although I give some overall frequencies here, for some of the verbal categories—with our very young children—there are insufficient examples to merit presenting frequencies for each category.

So throughout the book, while the children's remarks are often funny, sometimes poignant, they are not intended merely to amuse or divert but to highlight more general findings. Rather than belaboring the point, I shall quote an earlier writer who made it trenchantly. In 1798 Maria Edgeworth, in her *Practical Education,* a refreshingly sensible book on childrearing (full of illuminating observations based largely on her own fourteen children), tells the reader rather sternly that, in order to set before the public the results of her experiments, she was often "obliged to record facts concerning children which may seem trifling, and to enter into a minuteness of detail which may appear unnecessary. No anecdotes, however, have been admitted without due deliberation; nothing has been introduced to gratify the idle curiosity of others, or to indulge our own feelings of domestic partiality" (p. vi).

The studies I draw on for this book were supported by the Medical Research Council in Great Britain. I would like to thank the families of Cambridge who took part for their generous help, interest, and patience. I have changed the names of the children to ensure their anonymity. The studies were conducted in collaboration with Penny Munn, whose enthusiastic, thoughtful commitment to the project was indispensable. Much of the book was written while I was a Fellow at the Center for Advanced Study in the Bahvioral Sciences, Stanford University, with a grant from the John D. and Catherine T. MacArthur Foundation, and I am very grateful for that opportunity and for the many good discussions I had with other Fellows, especially John Darley and Richard Shweder.

Contents

The Beginnings of Social Understanding

1

Understanding Others?

There is nothing for which nature seems to have given us such a bent as for society.

—Montaigne, *Essays,* 1580

Children are born into a complex social world: from infancy on, they are active participants in a world of other people—adults and children, familiar and not-so-familiar others. On commonsense grounds it seems reasonable to argue that it is important for them to begin to understand the intentions, feelings, and actions of others who share their world and to comprehend the social rules of that world.

Yet when we come to consider the beginnings of this understanding—apparently of such adaptive importance that it would be high on the developmental agenda—we face a paradox. From research on infancy we know that babies are born predisposed to learn about sounds and sights that are characteristic features of *people*. They are particularly attentive to shapes and patterns that are like faces and to sounds that fall in the frequency range of the female human voice. As babies they learn especially fast about stimuli that change in a way that is contingent upon their own behavior—just as in real life people do. At two months old, they distinguish a person who intends to communicate with them from one who speaks to someone else (Trevarthen, 1977). Studies of the development of the ability of infants to perceive that the person one sees is the person one hears, and that certain visual and sound patterns specify the same individual, show that "Infants appear to possess innately, or to develop quickly, remarkable abilities to perceive the actions and expressions of other people" (Spelke and Cortelyou, 1981).

By the time they are seven to eight months old, we know that babies are tuned in to the different emotional expressions of adults. In situations of uncertainty, they monitor the emotional expressions of their mothers and respond differently, and appropriately, to those expressions (Klinnert et al., 1983). If they observe their mothers interacting positively with a stranger, they are less wary of that stranger subsequently than babies whose mothers interact neutrally (Feiring, Lewis, and Starr, 1984). They are sensitive to the direction of gaze of another person and seem to try to look in the same direction (Scaife and Bruner, 1975). As Rochelle Gelman and Elizabeth Spelke comment, "Infants as well as adults attempt to discover what others are doing or feeling" (1981, p. 51). At about nine months they notice the congruence between their own affective state and the affective expression on someone else's face (McKain et al., 1985). By this age, too, they are beginning to cooperate effectively with others in games (peekaboo, hide-and-seek) and in the familiar routines of being fed, changed, and dressed.

Most strikingly, babies are beginning to share a communicative framework of gestures and signals with others, waving goodbye appropriately when someone leaves, signaling their own requests with gestures shared by all family members. And this ability to understand and use a common communicative framework is particularly clear in infants' attempts to make their wishes and needs clear. As Jerome Bruner comments, their means to an end quickly includes the actions of other people, and "the infant's principal 'tool' for achieving his ends is another person" (1983). Babies are highly social, sociable creatures.

If, however, we ask about older children's ability to understand the emotions, perceptions, and intentions of other people, we find that research into perspective-taking tells us that children develop these abilities relatively slowly. This is the paradox. These abilities are apparently crucial for the individual, central to human evolution—yet they appear to develop, according to one tradition in developmental psychology, relatively slowly. When children of four, five, or six are faced with tasks that require them to take the perspective of others, or to make judgments about the feelings of people in stories or films (the experimental paradigm that psychologists have usually employed to understand the growth of these abilities), they often have real difficulties (Shantz, 1983). The original Piagetian picture of children as "egocentric" until they are six or seven has, of course, been drastically changed with experimental studies showing that the design of the tests crucially affects the abilities of the children to take the perspective of others. A developmental change from ignoring to being able to share a perspective can be demonstrated to take place at dramatically different ages—at eighteen months, at two and a half years, at four or even at ten years—according to the task and setting chosen (Flavell, 1985). But this research tells little about the nature of children's capabilities in the setting of their daily family life or about how these change with development.

So do children not develop these all-important capabilities until well after infancy? Do we conclude that for a child the crucial development of becoming human—the understanding that other people have feelings and minds like his or her own, yet also different—is extremely slow? Children develop their powers of communication, understanding, and thought, their emotional security and their sense of themselves, within a complex social framework: do they nevertheless fail to grasp the nature of the moods, interests, and relationships of others who share that world, or the ground rules of that world, until they are five or seven years old? When and how do children begin to understand the feelings and intentions of other people, the social rules and roles of the world in which they grow up?

Piaget and Sullivan argued that in the "decentering" processes by which children overcome difficulties in understanding others, it is the arguments and disagreements between five- or six-year-olds that are of key importance. In these disputes, they suggested, children are forced for the first time to take account of the differing views and perspectives of another person (Piaget, 1932; Sullivan, 1953). What then of the period between infancy and this stage of the disputes between articulate school-age children, who impel each other to face one another's point of view? How do children behave in the world of the family, if their social understanding is indeed so very limited?

Here we face a gap. There is a wealth of research on the first year of life, research that beautifully documents the nature of infants' social behavior, their fine-tuned responsiveness to the behavior and moods of other people (see for example Stern, 1985). There is also a flourishing tradition of research on the capability (and incapability) of school-age children to take the perspective of others, and on their developing ideas about friendship, authority, and justice (Damon, 1977; Selman, 1980; Youniss, 1980). Between these two fields of research, in the period of the transition from infancy to childhood, there is a relatively unexplored area. It is unexplored in part because the development of social intelligence has only recently become a matter of interest to developmental psychologists concerned with the second and third years of childhood. While clinicians have long been concerned with the infant's developing sense of identity and autonomy over this age period (Mahler, Pine, and Bergman, 1975), for developmental psychologists it is the dramatic developments in acquisition of language and symbolic representation, of communicative skills and categorization of the object world, that have held center stage. These do of course have profound implications for the development of children's social intelligence. But with the notable exception of those interested in the pragmatics of early language, and of a small group of psychologists interested in young children's "theories of mind," psychologists studying the acquisition of language or conceptual development have not been primarily concerned with the nature of children's understanding of their social world.

Moreover, the development of human social understanding and communication involves a wide range of abilities in addition to the acquisition of syntax or even semantics. People do not simply cue each other into propositional exchanges: they communicate their moods and desires, their sense of absurdity and amusement, disapproval, pride or shame. They communicate shared beliefs about the way life should be lived and about relationships between the members of their world in a variety of subtle and not-so-subtle ways. To become a *person*—a member of that complex world—children must develop powers of recognizing and sharing emotional states, of interpreting and anticipating others' reactions, of understanding the relationships between others, of comprehending the sanctions, prohibitions, and accepted practices of their world. We have learned much of the nature of social and emotional communication in infancy from laboratory studies, but on children's understanding of their social world, our information is very sketchy. Why should this be?

Our ignorance is in part a result of the way in which developmental psychology has grown and is practiced. Children have rarely been studied in the world in which these developments take place, or in a context in which we can be sensitive to the subtleties of their social understanding. Psychology has developed as an experimental science, with all the strengths of precision and of causal explanation that this implies, but also with the consequence that the developments within the complex emotional world of the family have been neglected (with the notable exception of language acquisition). In domains such as the development of numeracy or logical reasoning, changes in children's cognitive capacity in the early years have come under stringent scrutiny, with elegant experimental studies (Gelman and Baillargeon, 1983; Markman, 1981). But developments in social understanding are less amenable to experimental investigation with very young children. Open a textbook on developmental psychology and look for the sections on preschool children's social behavior: you will probably find a section on the attachment of child to parent (and this may well be a discussion of the relationship only in terms of the behavior of the child when separated from the parent in a fifteen-minute laboratory assessment) and a section on behavior with peers (usefully accessible to the psychologist in a daycare center or playgroup). These are centrally important features of children's social behavior. But what about the children's relationships within the world in which they grow up and their understanding of that world—a world in which the relationship between parent and child is very much more than what we can hope to capture in the laboratory "strange situation," a world shared with grandparents, friends, neighbors, and siblings?

Some of the research currently being carried out on children's communication, their understanding of mental phenomena and their symbolic play, is clearly relevant to the beginnings of social understanding. Most strikingly, studies of how children use language show that children begin to understand the *intentions* behind speech very early. Bruner (1983) very clearly presents the argument that, before the child is a skilled language user, he has learned something of what is "canonical, obligatory, and valued" in his culture. He knows, for instance, a great deal about the cultural conditions of requesting a year before he knows how to apply the grammatical inversion rule for framing a question. And in achieving the skills of referential or requesting communication, children have begun to coordinate their language and actions with those of other people in ways that are culturally prescribed.

But the course of development of that cultural understanding in the second and third year remains unclear. We do know that children in the second year become increasingly aware of adult standards, from Jerome Kagan's pioneering work (1981). We also know something of children's sensitivity to the emotional states of others during this period, from the work of early psychologists (see Chapters 5 and 6) and from the more recent work of Radke-Yarrow, Zahn-Waxler, and their colleagues. Their studies have shown that during the second year children's responses to the distress of others become increasingly differentiated, and their ability to comfort increasingly effective (Zahn-Waxler and Radke-Yarrow, 1982). The same researchers have demonstrated that if children of this age witness angry quarrels between adults, they get very upset and are themselves more likely to be aggressive. This interest that children show in emotions is documented too in studies of children's verbal references to feeling states. Children begin to talk about their own and other peoples' feelings toward the end of the second year and do so with increasing differentiation and frequency during the third (Bretherton, McNew, and Beeghly-Smith, 1981; Dunn, Bretherton, and Munn, 1986).

A child's ability to talk about mental states—knowing, thinking, believing, remembering—develops later, during the third year (Shatz, Wellman, and Silber, 1983). The nature of three- and four-year-olds' growing understanding of "other minds" has been the focus of the research of Henry Wellman and his colleagues (Johnson and Wellman, 1982; Wellman, 1985, 1986; Wellman and Estes, 1986). These studies document the coherence in children's understanding of mental phenomena and their grasp of the causes of human action in terms of beliefs, desires, and intentions. Wellman, while pinpointing the deficiencies in their "theory of mind," argues that conversations of children at home show that children even younger than those who have been studied experimentally have an understanding of human action that is fundamentally akin to adult folk psychology: "It shares, in principle if not in detail, the basic belief-desire-intention framework for understanding human acts . . . this knowledge is coherent, rests on and mandates crucial ontological distinctions, and is centrally tied to a causal-explanatory framework" (1986, p. 23).

The focus of this work is the early development of explicit knowledge of the mind in children as they reach their third birthday and beyond. Wellman's argument fits well with other evidence for children's interest in the causes of human behavior, notably the analyses by Lois Bloom and her colleagues of children's early causal comments and questions (Bloom and Capatides, 1987; Hood and Bloom, 1979). These show that children's early essays into discussion of cause are focused on *psychological* causality; they are about why people act the way they do, about how sociocultural practices, emotions, and judgments are reasons for actions.

This picture of the interest in human behavior that three-year-olds demonstrate within the family links in an important and convincing fashion with what we know of four-year-olds' understanding of mental phenomena and the social world. For instance Susan Carey, studying conceptual change in children between four and twelve years old, has drawn attention to what she terms children's "intuitive psychology," an explanatory system in which wants and beliefs account for actions. She shows that such a "theory" is well established by the age of four. And other experimental research has certainly demonstrated that four–five-year-olds have the ability to understand and talk about phenomena such as intentions and false beliefs (Schulz, 1980; Wimmer and Perner, 1983). But what, Carey asks, is the origin of this intuitive psychology? Her own guess is "that infants are endowed with the tools to build an intuitive psychology, just as they are endowed with the tools to build an intuitive mechanics and a human language" (1985, p. 200). Whether or not this guess is correct, she comments, is an important issue for those who seek explanatory theories of learning. From a very different perspective, Barbara Tizard and Martin Hughes (1985), studying the conversations of four-year-olds at home with their mothers, have given us a vivid picture of the children's curiosity and logical powers, one that highlights the remarkable breadth of interest that four-year-olds show in their social world.

Research into the development of children's make-believe amplifies our picture of the beginnings of social understanding. Studies of children's solitary play with "replica" objects and dolls demonstrate how in their pretend play they begin to represent two-party interactions with simple narratives involving different roles (Nicholich, 1975). Note, however, that while children's doll play is a favorite context for developmentalists and clinicians, it is not clear precisely how children's enactment of social situations and narratives with dolls relates to their understanding of people in real life, a point that Dennie Wolf has emphasized. According to her detailed study of a boy growing from infant to toddler, the child's understanding of others' agency and experience surfaces *later* in his doll play than in his own goal-directed actions (Wolf, 1982). The question of how and when we should use children's play narratives to examine their understanding of other people and events remains an open one, and one that is important to explore.

It should be noted, too, that much of this research on symbolic development in play has focused on a solitary child, playing alone with toys. We get a rather different picture of the development of the ability to represent others from studying children playing with their mother, siblings, or familiar peers. It has been clearly argued by those studying social play in the second year, and children's first essays into sociodramatic play, that such play shows us that "the foundations for interpersonal understanding" have been laid (Wolf, 1984). Yet studies of the earliest stages of children's abilities to enact and play with social roles and rules, developments that take place within the family in the second year, are still few and far between (but see Miller and Garvey, 1984; Dunn and Dale, 1984; Wolf, 1984).

Studies of the "scripts" that children acquire for their familiar daily routines are also important and relevant, although this research has not yet considered children's knowledge of feelings and relationships. And both in research into the mother-child attachment and in the growing literature on the early stages of children's sense of themselves, there is increasing interest in the question of how children respond to and understand their social world—interest, but little systematic study. In research on the attachment of child to mother, for example, theorists are now increasingly interested in exploring Bowlby's notion of the infant's "working model" of the mother and urge that we should turn our attention to understanding the infant's subjective experience of the relationship (Bretherton, 1985). In research on the development of sense of self, it is implicit, but rarely explicitly examined, that children's understanding of others develops along with their sense of self. Daniel Stern's work (1985), for instance, gives us an illuminating picture of the central part that developments in affective understanding and communication play in the child's developing sense of self; yet here, as in most writing on developments in the first and second year within a clinical framework, the focus is on changing conceptions of *self* rather than on children's conceptions of *others*.

What this exciting work on children's language, affective communication, play, conceptual development, and developing sense of self gives us is an impetus to look further at the nature of children's growing understanding of their social world, at how this is employed in and influences their relationships. With the few notable exceptions I have mentioned, there is little published study of the nature of children's understanding of others' emotions and intentions, of social rules, or of relationships between others in their own social world during the transition from infancy to childhood. The suggestion that children may in fact reflect on moral and social issues or on the feelings of others very early in development is sometimes tentatively made, as in the reflective essay on children's understanding of the distinction between animate and inanimate objects by Gelman and Spelke (1981), where they comment that "children may think in terms of the permissibility or the morality of actions at an early age." Similarly, Hoffman, writing on children's understanding of people and things, suggests from one anecdote: "If we may generalize tentatively from this instance, it would appear that some kind of rapid processing of information about other people's feelings, at least in familiar, highly motivating natural settings, is possible in children still in the sensory-motor period as regards the physical domain" (1981, p. 72).

The suggestions are tentative because the information is anecdotal. And our ideas on the processes underlying the developments in understanding over this period remain vague. From our textbooks we are left with the picture of one- and two-year-old children as largely incapable of reflecting upon the feelings and intentions of others, struggling with the crises of developing autonomy, individuation, and separation from the mother. To ask questions about the nature of such egocentric creatures' understanding of other people and of social rules seems quite inappropriate.

But if we set aside the textbook account and look at children in the world in which they grow up, the relevance of such questions about social intelligence is inescapable. This book examines the nature of that social intelligence and its development. The concern is not to claim simply that children's capabilities develop six, twelve, or twenty-four months earlier than previously thought. Rather, the argument is about why and how children develop powers of social and moral understanding, about the relation between those powers and their social relationships, their sense of self, their driving self-interest, and their emotional experiences. I should emphasize at the outset that my focus on the children's emotions, motivation, and relationships does not imply a dismissal of cognitive mechanisms in the development of social understanding. Their importance is taken as a given. But the studies I shall describe suggest that the prevailing concentration on cognitive mechanisms as *independent* of emotional and motivational factors may not be providing the most useful framework for thinking about the development of social understanding.

My argument is developed by examining in turn a number of different facets of children's social behavior and relationships: their disputes, arguments, and behavior in conflict, their empathetic and cooperative behavior, their discussion of other people, their ability to take part in family conversation, their fantasy play and jokes. To make inferences about what children understand from a tally of the words they say without regard to their functional use, or from single isolated incidents of behavior, or from their pretend play alone, would clearly be hazardous and unwise. My strategy is to consider the children's behavior and speech in a variety of contexts, with different partners and in different emotional settings. I draw in part on the research of other developmental psychologists, in part on the writings and observations of those who have studied children in earlier times (whose observations are valuable because they study children within the family), but primarily on three longitudinal studies of families that my colleagues and I have carried out in Cambridge. Let us begin, after a brief look at the studies, with the children themselves, fighting, playing, talking—with the daily dramas of family life in which their powers of social intelligence are revealed and fostered.

2

Confronting the Mother

Tis wonderful to observe how very early a Wilfulness is discernable in Children; and with what progress it gather strength.

—James Nelson, *Essay on the Government of Children*, 1753

The children we studied were all growing up in Cambridge, England, or in neighboring villages, some in working-class and others in middle-class families. Most lived on estates of council (public) housing or in semidetached turn-of-the-century houses, with their parents and siblings. At the start of the studies, none of the mothers was in full-time employment outside the home during the day, though many worked part-time. Although the social class of the families, in terms of the fathers' occupation, was varied, the pattern of the young children's lives was in some respects quite similar. There was a common routine of close contact with the mother as chief caregiver, outings to local shops, parks, and playgrounds, and frequent contact with other children (friends of the older sibling or neighboring children). Few of the mothers had the use of a car, so for most children life was centered on the housing estate or neighborhood. Play space and toys were plentiful for most children: the houses usually had a large living room in which the family ate meals, watched television, and the mothers talked with neighbors, did the ironing, or sorted and mended clothes.

In other respects, family routines and rules differed. In some families meals were rarely taken by the whole family together at the table; in others the children were expected to sit through a family meal. Attitudes toward tidiness, sharing, and manners all varied. Aggression and quarreling, however, were frowned on by all the mothers, though their attempts to control the level of conflict between their children varied in style and intensity, as did the disputes between the children. Common to all the children we studied was an increasing expectation, during their second and third years, that they would begin to "fit in" with the pattern of family rules—and a growing pressure on them to comply.

Our aim was to observe the children at home with as little disruption of their daily life as possible. Inevitably an observer's presence affects the ways in which family members behave. We tried to minimize this in a variety of ways: we did not remain silent and unresponsive if the children and mothers spoke to us, the same observer visited each family at each visit, the visits were relatively frequent and extensive. The frequency of fights, arguments, and extended fantasy play episodes during the observations suggests that our presence did not damp down the children unduly. Details of the sample and the methods we used are given in the appendix. In brief, we employed a combination of methods, including detailed precoded categories of behavior that were recorded on a ten-second time base, narrative notes, and audio-tape recording of the children's conversations using a small recorder. Our first study followed six families over the second child's second year in some detail, visiting the families when the secondborn children were 14, 16, 18, 21, 24, and 36 months old (Study 1); the second followed forty families, visiting when the secondborn children were 18, 24, and 36 months old (Study 2); the third followed six families over the third year, visiting when the children were 24, 26, 28, 30, 33, and 36 months old (Fig. 2.1).

With these overlapping studies we were able to look in detail

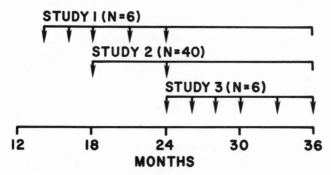

Fig. 2.1 Timing of visits (Studies 1, 2, and 3)

at developments in the second and third year and also examine how general these patterns were with the data from the forty children of Study 2. At each time point in all studies we made two hour-long observations. Occasional mention will be made of a fourth study, in which we followed families from before the birth of a second child through the infancy of the second child (Study 4: Dunn and Kendrick, 1982).

The next three chapters consider the question of how children's behavior in conflict with their mothers and siblings can illuminate the nature of their social understanding. We observe the children arguing, teasing, and making excuses, to see what light this throws on the children's comprehension of the feelings and wishes of another person, on their grasp of the dynamics of family relationships, and of what is acceptable and unacceptable within the family. In this chapter and the next, descriptive accounts of distinctive features of the children's behavior when they are faced with the opposition of mother or sibling are given, and in Chapter 4 the implications of these observations for our ideas on the development of social understanding are discussed.

Assertiveness and emotion

Throughout the last three centuries doctors, diarists, and philosophers writing about children and childrearing have noted the growth of willful, disobedient, and contrary behavior in the second and third years of life. The passion and the pleasure children show in resisting parental wishes is documented—often with anguish—by parents and by those concerned with the moral development of children. Our observations of the Cambridge children followed through the transition from infancy to childhood confirm the accuracy of the accounts given by these earlier writers. And three themes stand out from these observations: the *emotion* that the children show—anger or delight when confronting their parents; the *understanding* that their behavior reveals—understanding of the feelings of others and of the rules of the family; and the *self-interest* that drives much of their behavior. It is the significance of the relations between these three themes that forms an important thread in the argument of this book, and I begin with the evidence for each of these in the children's interaction with their mothers.

The evidence for the growth of assertive and resistant behavior shown by the children toward their mothers was striking. While exchanges in which the mother simply prohibited the child and the child complied without protest occurred at much the same frequency as the children grew from 14-month-olds to three-year-olds (on average, around nine such exchanges for each two hours of observation), conflicts in which the child protested the mother's actions, resisted her demands, or—most irritating of all for the mothers—repeated what they had just been forbidden to do all nearly doubled in frequency between 18 and 24 months. The children's assertiveness was shown too in the way in which they persisted in demands that the mother had refused. The majority of the children in Study 2—32 out of 40—behaved in this deliberately resistant way.

Evident too was the emotion of many of the children during these episodes. Displays of anger—angry faces and voices, destruction of objects, self-injury, full-blown tantrums—were relatively rare in conflict with the mother at 14 months but increased significantly over the months that followed (Dunn and Munn, 1985). This sharp increase in angry outbursts directed at the mother was graphically described in a study carried out in the 1930s by Frances Goodenough (Fig. 2.2). Distress also peaked at 24 months in our Cambridge children. The point of emphasizing the increase in anger and distress here is not to claim a new discovery. The drama created by the angry two-year-old has been commented on for centuries. Rather, I want to draw attention to this increase in emotional behavior because of its possible role in the children's developing understanding. The emotion experienced in these exchanges may well influence what the child *learns* during such interactions.

Anger and distress were not the only emotions that the children expressed during disputes with their mothers. With steadily increasing frequency during the second year, the children smiled and laughed during confrontations (Dunn and Munn, 1985).

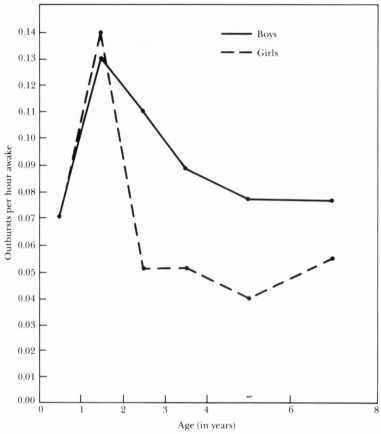

Fig. 2.2 Frequency of angry outbursts in the home, from Goodenough (1931)

Many of these exchanges had a deliberate teasing quality, as this
example illustrates.

1. Family E (Study 1). Child 18 months
Child sitting on mother's knee, pulls M's hair hard.

M: Don't pull my hair! Madam! Don't pull hair. No. It's not
nice to pull hair, is it?
C: Hair.
M: Hair, yes, but you mustn't pull it, must you?

C: Yes! (smiles).
M: No! No!
C: No!
M: No. No. It's not kind to pull hair, is it?
C: Nice! (smiles).
M: No, it isn't.
C: Nice!

In such exchanges the children often appeared intentionally to upset their mothers—and to enjoy the consequences of their actions. What is important here is that the children seem to anticipate their mothers' feeling state and get pleasure from the power to affect them in this way.

Amusement and sometimes out-and-out delight were shown not only in the direct confrontations between child and mother, but in more indirect transgressions. In Study 1 we recorded the children's looking behavior in some detail; the results revealed that there was a steady increase over the second year in the frequency with which the children looked at their mothers or the observer and smiled or laughed, when carrying out a previously forbidden action.

2. Family B (Study 1). Child 18 months
Child heads for electric socket, forbidden twice during
last 20 minutes of observation. Turns to look at
observer, smiling.

Such incidents are familiar to all parents of children of this age; they may seem trivial, but they do indicate that the children are already by 18 months beginning to anticipate their mothers' response to forbidden actions and finding this situation a source of pleasure. Their attention to the observer also suggests some expectation that familiar adults are likely to behave in similar ways to what is forbidden. That children of this age have some conception of what is frowned on by the mother is not startling. Dogs, after all, show much the same anticipation of their owners' stern disapproval when they turn over the garbage in search of good things. We shall return to this later, but for the moment note the pleasure and excitement the children show as they deliberately repeat the forbidden act, and note their behavior with the familiar observer. Their pleasure in transgression brings us to the question of their understanding of what is acceptable within the family.

Awareness of adult standards and others' feelings

Attention, evasion, and deceit

The children did not always look and smile when carrying out forbidden actions. Two other patterns of behavior commonly occurred in the first months of the second year. First, they sometimes drew their mothers' attention to the forbidden action or to its results:

3. Family B (Study 1). Child 16 months
Child takes sibling's bag of candy (previously forbidden), carries it to M.

M: Yes. You've got Molly's bag of sweets haven't you? Not yours, is it? You'll be in trouble.

4. Family H (Study 1) Child 16 months
Child has opened M's handbag and removed several items. Takes two to M.

M: What have you got there?
C: (vocalizes).
M: Yes. Two things you didn't ought to have. Are you going to give them to Mummy?
C: (shakes head).
M: Ta! (instruction to hand over, slang for "thank you").
C: (shakes head).
M: Ta! Are you going to? Ta! Give them to Mummy then (takes them from her). You knew you weren't supposed to, didn't you, Miss?

5. Family H (Study 1). Child 16 months
Child spills M's drink, vocalizes, looks at M and points
to spill.

M: Done it again, have you?

By 18 months each of the children in Study 1 had been
observed to behave in this way. Such behavior was often apparently unemotional; these youngsters did not have the expressions of shame or guilt evident in older children when their
misdemeanors are discovered. Instead they seemed to be checking out the results of their actions. And the mothers responded
in almost every instance with verbal comments, often discussing
cause and consequence and usually making some reference to
the unacceptability of the child's behavior. Sometimes the children appeared to tease their mothers over the incident: in the
next example Martin draws his mother's attention to the milk
he has spilled by commenting that it is the moon.

6. Family C (Study 1). Child 21 months
Child spills milk, shows it to M.

C: Look. Look. Look. Moon. There moon. Moon.
M: Where's the moon?
C: ——(inaudible) a moon. ——a moon. There sunshine.
M: It's not! It's milk on the carpet.
C (smiling): Goodbye! (To observer) More mess! More mess!

The second common pattern following an action that has been
forbidden seemed to involve deliberate evasion of the mother.

7. Family H (Study 1). Child 18 months
Child has stitches in her forehead as the result of a fall
the previous day. In the course of the observation she
"discovers" the stitches and begins to pull at them. M
prohibits her and attempts to distract. After a few minutes the child feels for the stitches and is stopped again.

Three minutes later she goes behind the settee and pulls at the stitches.

There were also incidents during the second half of the second year in which the child's behavior appeared to be a deliberate attempt to mislead the mother, in order for the child to get her way. In the next example Ellie has made several requests to play with soap, which her mother repeatedly refused. When her mother finally says she can have it later in the bath, Ellie lies on the floor with her legs in the air—the position in which her diaper is changed—and indicates that she needs cleaning (she is in fact quite clean).

8. Family H (Study 1). Child 21 months
Child and M in bathroom. Child points to soap with request vocalization.

M: Have a bath later, shall we?
C: Ba.
M: You put it in the bath, ready then?
C: (does so).
M: There you are. Now it's ready for you later when you have a bath. Come on.
C: Ba (points to soap).
M: No, we're not taking it. I said you can get in the bath later.
C: (lies down on floor in position for diaper change and gestures to diaper).
M: No, I'm not taking it off.
C: Cack (word for dirty diaper).
M: No, you haven't.
C: Cack.
M: No, you haven't.

Note that this 21-month-old demonstrates remarkably sophisticated behavior in the service of her own interest: she wants to get the prized soap.
The same general point is illustrated in the next example,

another incident that involves an attempt to achieve a desired end through pretense or, less euphemistically, deceit. Sally, a very energetic girl of 24 months, was bouncing around the room but, when refused a piece of chocolate cake she spied on the table, whined that she was tired. She apparently (and correctly) assumed that the state of tiredness would provide her a better chance of being given food.

9. *Family T (Study 2). Child 24 months*
Child sees chocolate cake on table.

C: Bibby on.
M: You don't want your bibby on. You're not eating.
C: Chocolate cake. Chocolate cake.
M: You're not having any chocolate cake either.
C: Why? (whines) Tired.
M: You tired? Ooh!
C: Chocolate cake.
M: No chance.

The attempt fails but is a striking example of how children of only 24 months can pretend to be in a state other than their own, if it is in their interest to do so.

Again, every dogowner can probably cap such incidents with an account of how a pet deliberately evaded punishment by anticipation of the owner's action or appeared intentionally to mislead the owner into acting in some desired way. The early writers have noted that deceitful behavior begins to appear in the second half of the second year (for instance, Stern, 1924). James Sully (1896), the father of the child-study movement and a careful observer of children, describes several instances:

C. on being asked by his mother who told him something, answered "Dolly." False, and knowingly false, somebody will say, especially when he learns that the depraved youngster instantly proceeded to laugh . . .
When seventeen and a half months old she threw down her

gloves when wheeled in her mail cart by her mother. The latter picked them up and told her not to throw them away again. She was at first good, them seemed to deliberate and finally called out: "Mamma, Bubbo" (dog). The mother turned to look, and the little imp threw her gloves away again, laughing; there was of course no dog ... About two months later, after she had thrown down and broken her tea-things, and her mother had come up to her, she said: "Mamma broke tea-things—beat Mamma", and proceeded to beat her. (pp. 254, 258)

Children's interest in (perhaps exploration of) what is approved and what is not permitted behavior within the family is one strand of a broader concern that the children showed in standards—or, rather, in objects or behavior that deviated from normal or accepted standards. This awareness of standards was evident not only in emotional disputes with mothers but also in less acrimonious exchanges, as the following section illustrates.

Dirt, untidiness, and things that are spoiled

If we can abstract pathogenicity and hygiene from our notion of dirt, we are left with the old definition of dirt as matter out of place. This is a very suggestive approach. It implies two conditions: a set of ordered relations and a contravention of that order. Dirt, then, is never a unique isolated event. Where there is dirt there is system. Dirt is the by-product of a systematic ordering and classifying of matter, in so far as ordering involves rejecting inappropriate elements. (Douglas, 1966, p. 35)

Our society's concern about dirt and untidiness clearly mirrors our classification of what is acceptable, as Mary Douglas argues in *Purity and Danger*. To examine young children's interest in dirt and untidiness can give us a useful window on their perspective on standards. It is an interest that grows strikingly during the second year. Jerome Kagan (1981) described children showing a concern about adult standards in experimental settings from 19 months on. The children in our first six-family study (Study 1) expressed, from 14 months on, increasingly frequent interest in objects that were broken, dirty, or out of place (Fig. 2.3), and they proceeded in turn to draw others' attention to them. Their concern was shown not only over broken and dirty things but over objects that were not in their usual place in the house or that were apparently being taken by people other than the rightful possessors. Clearly some notion of possession rules was reflected in this behavior—a notion that was unquestionably and vehemently demonstrated as far as their own belongings were concerned.

Our observations revealed two links between the children's growing concern with dirt or misplaced objects and the behavior of adults. First, the mothers themselves, from our earliest

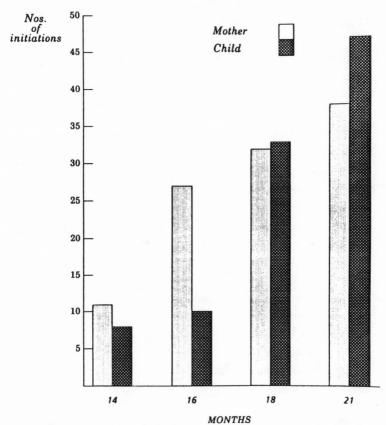

Fig. 2.3 Initiation of communication about broken/dirty/misplaced objects, by child and mother (Study 1)

observations onward, drew the children's attention to dirty, or flawed objects and did so with increasing frequency as the year progressed. Second, whether it was child or mother who had initiated the joint attention to the dirty, flawed, or out-of-place object, what followed was a conversation in which both mother and child discussed the issue.

10. Family N (Study 1). Child 16 months
Child in high chair, throws biscuit on floor.

M: What's that? Biscuit on the floor? Where biscuits aren't supposed to be? Isn't it?
C: (looks at M and nods).
M: Yes. Now what's all this? (points to toothbrush and toothpaste on kitchen table). Who brought that downstairs?
C: (looks at M and smiles).
M: Yes, you did. Where does that live?
C: Bath.

11. Family N (Study 1). Child 18 months
Child brings M toy frog with rip in its body, points to tear.

M: I think he's sprung a leak, hasn't he, John?
C: (points again to tear).
M: Oh yes. I see (tries to mend frog).
C: No.
M: Well, I'm trying to mend it.
C: Look (points again to frog).
M: Yes, it's mended.
C: No (shakes head).
M: It jolly well is mended.
C: (shakes head, points to further hole). Look.

In conversations like these, mothers frequently articulated for their children the ways in which the offending or interesting object failed to reach acceptable standards. Discussion of a toothbrush on the kitchen table, of a toy frog with a missing eye, or of spilt milk may seem too mundane and trivial to be of interest, concerned if we are with such grand issues as the development of social understanding. Yet, as Mary Douglas points out, such incidents are deeply revealing:

> We can recognise in our own notions of dirt that we are using a kind of omnibus compendium which includes all the rejected elements of ordered systems. It is a relative idea. Shoes are not dirty in themselves, but it is dirty to place them on the dining-table; food is not dirty in itself, but it is dirty to leave cooking utensils in the bedroom, or food bespattered on clothing; similarly, bathroom equipment in the drawing room; clothing lying on chairs; out-door things in-doors; upstairs things downstairs . . . In short, our pollution behaviour is the reaction which condemns any object or idea likely to confuse or contradict cherished classifications. (p. 36)

To the child of 18 months, shoes on the table are a source of interest and amusement with which to tease your mother. The pleasure shown at contradicting "cherished classifications" demonstrates the children's understanding of these classifications, their grasp of the *shared nature* of those classifications, and their understanding of how that knowledge can be used in relationships—used as a source of shared humor and as a strategy in combat with adults. Bathroom equipment in the kitchen is already at 20 months a matter for discussion and comment. Many of the everyday rules of family life are already understood; they are interesting not only in themselves but as a source of amusement and conflict. The child smiling at his mother's concern over the toothpaste on the kitchen table shows us his grasp of some of the ground rules of the family, his recognition that such rules are shared, as well as his enjoyment at using this understanding in the power play between mother and child.

Conversation and understanding the rules

It is evident from the examples given so far that a joint focus of child and mother on a transgression, a broken toy, or a misplaced object means a conversation about the issue. The conversational nature of such exchanges was striking, even when the children were only 14 months old and unable to talk themselves. Mothers frequently commented on the breach or the broken object in question form—and left "space" for the child to answer. And even as young as 16 months, the children began to take part in these conversations, with shakes of the head, nods, and smiles.

12. Family B (Study 1). Child 16 months
Child reaches for plugged-in iron.

M: Leave it, Mary. You mustn't pull it out, must you?
C: (shakes head).

By 18 and 20 months, the children were taking part more explicitly in an active way, playing, teasing, contradicting, and insisting on their own way verbally. Justifications and excuses for defiant behavior were given more and more frequently. At 24 months, children in the forty-family study gave reasons to excuse their actions in 11 percent of the conflicts with their mothers; by 36 months, excuses were given in 32 percent of such conflicts (Fig. 2.4)—a significant increase (Appendix Table 1). Their arguments make it clear that at a practical level they have grasped the idea of prescriptivity and the possibility of breach and sanction. A closer look at the children's comments, justifications, and excuses begins to give us a picture of their moral intuitions: their notions of harm or injury to others, of responsibility, of what exempts an individual from the application of a rule, and so on. Beyond this picture of the child as moralist, we can see in such conversations how the child *uses* this growing understanding in his family relationships, to get his way, to escape blame, to deflect punishment onto his sibling, to tease and joke—the child as psychologist.

The idea of harm to others

Our children commented on and explored the consequences of particular actions for other's feelings. Their grasp of the con-

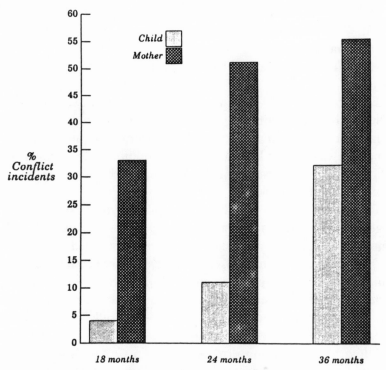

Fig. 2.4 Proportion of conflict incidents in which child and mother reason/justify their actions (Study 2)

nection between their own action and another person's pain was clear.

13. Family H (Study 1). Child 24 months
Child sitting on M's knee, kicks her.

M: Don't kick because that hurts.
C: More hurt (repeats kick).
M: No!
C: More hurt (repeats kick).

14. Family M (Study 2). Child 24 months
Child accidentally knocks baby sibling (Thomas), who cries. M enters room.

C: Poor Thomas.
M: What happened?
C: I banged him.
M: Well, you'd better kiss him better.

Recall, too, the little girl pulling her mother's hair (example 1). The deliberate repetition of an action that causes pain is a theme that recurs particularly often in the interactions between siblings, as we shall see later. But mothers do not escape altogether, though, as in the case of the hair pulling, such actions are more often playful than hostile.

The evidence for children's developing understanding of agency—their own and that of other people—during the latter months of the first year has been lucidly reviewed by Dennie Wolf (1982). What our observations show here is that children understand that people can cause pain to others. It is not yet a wide or differentiated notion of harm: indeed, explicit verbal comments are limited, among the two-year-olds, to references to physical harm (although they know well how to tease psychologically, they don't discuss such pain verbally). But in this limited sense, the principal of harm to others is understood—and it is an essential foundation for understanding moral rules, a sine qua non for moral sensibility.

The idea of responsibility

In the second and third year, children are also beginning to understand the idea of responsibility—that individuals are not only agents in causing pain but are accountable to others for such prohibited actions. In the example of the little girl's comments on her brother's distress after she banged him, the link between her action and his crying is only implicit in her utterances. But explicit discussion of responsibility for breaches of rules (and indeed the occasional use of moral terms to comment on behavior) does begin to appear toward the end of the second year. By 21 months, as we have noted, children are aware that spilt milk is a breach of the acceptable. Even if not something to cry over, it is something that will bring attention, reproval, and immediate attempts to remedy. Martin, the little boy in the next example, comments on his responsibility for a result that he knows to be a breach of conduct (see also his behavior in example 6—in both incidents there is a teasing quality to his delighted announcement).

15. Family C (Study 1). Child 21 months
Child spills milk on floor, looks at M.

M: Oh dear, oh dear!
C: Look!
M: Look! Yes!
C (rubbing at spill with hand): Rub it in. Rub it in. (To observer) I done it. I done it.

Later, during the third year, we see that children are indeed moving toward an understanding of accountability, as supported by their blaming of others and the denial of their own culpability.

16. Family A (Study 3). Child 30 months
Child (Annie) and sibling (Carol) are playing with hose
in garden, previously forbidden. Child turns it on again.

C to sib: And it got some water out spraying.
Sib to C: Make some out of this (pulls other end of hose).
M enters garden: Who's put the hosepipe out again?
C to M: Carol.
Sib to M: No it was Annie.
M to both: Why did any of you put the hosepipe out again?
   'Cos I'd packed it all away to go in the shed.
C to M: Umm. Carol did it.
S: I didn't. She did it.
C to M: Carol did it.
Sib to C: No she didn't. (to M:) Oh no I didn't. She done it.
C to M: Carol did. Carol did.

.

Sib to C (shouts): I did not!!
C to M: Umm. Carol——
M to both: Well, whoever it was is a naughty girl.
Sib to M: It was Annie.

17. Family J (Study 3). Child 30 months
Mother of child (Jay) and his older brother (Len) discovers mark on wall and attempts to rub it off.

M to C: Was it you?
C: Huh?
M: Was it you?
C: No. I think Len done it.

Often such acts of denial or blame are made in situations where it is transparently obvious that the child is in fact the culprit. No very elaborate sophistication in covering tracks is shown. But the denials indicate that the children have some anticipation of the mother's likely action, and some foresight about evasive action more elaborate than simply disappearing behind the sofa (an action frequently taken as a 16-20-month-old). Understanding the notion of responsibility implies a conception of *self* in relation to a conception of the *good*; the first steps toward that conception are evident here.

The use of moral terms to label those responsible for transgressions by the mothers was often observed during the second year. More surprising was the use of such items by the children before they were two.

18. Family H (Study 1). Child 21 months
Child (Ella), in highchair at table, throws toy on floor (previously forbidden), looks at M.

M: No! What's Ella?
C: Bad bad Baba.
M: A bad bad Baba.

What Ella understands by the term "bad" here is of course obscure. It is probable that this little conversation is a routine exchange, a ritual that she and her mother go through frequently during the day, when forbidden acts are repeated. But even if in the early stages the terms used in such routines do not mean much to the child, it is possible that such ritualized exchanges play a considerable part in the growth of the child's understanding. It has been argued, indeed, that it is in the context of such familiar repeated exchanges that children make important advances in their understanding and use of language. For the moment let us simply note that such exchanges were familiar to the child, following her frequent deliberate opposition to her mother.

A principle of justice?

The children understood that their actions led to breaches of acceptable behavior, such as harm to others, destruction, and mess. They also understood that justifications or excuses for such breaches could be given, and one set of such excuses shows us that in their third year they had begun to grasp the notion that the rules of acceptable behavior apply differently to different people. We hold that to be just or fair is not necessarily to treat all individuals alike. Indeed, although the central idea behind the principle of justice is that "what is right (or wrong) for one is right (or wrong) for any similar person in similar circumstances" (Singer, 1963, p. 19), this is in itself incomplete as a guide to conduct. Groups of people resemble each other in some ways and differ in others, and the maxim "Treat like cases alike" is not useful unless we know what dimensions of resemblance are relevant or important (Hart, 1961).

Excuses of lack of control. Among the excuses the children used during the third year were claims of incapacity and of pretend identity. In their claims to be babies, the children made clear that they understood that what is expected of a baby is different from what is expected of a two-year-old. Jay, the child who blamed his brother in example 17 above, in the same observation attempted to get his mother to hold him and, when she refused, said of himself, "He's a baby, Mummy. He can't walk." In our first sibling study we found that, after the birth of a sibling, the firstborn children often pretended to be babies when their mothers asked them to help or to clean up a mess they had made; one three-year-old first pretended to be his baby brother, then shifted to being a baby himself, in order to avoid helping his mother clean up (Dunn and Kendrick, 1982). Related to these excuses based on the incapacity of babies, and their consequent exemption from the rules that govern older children, were the frequent claims, in response to instructions to help parents, that "I can't. I can't do it."

Children also attempted to be excused from the application of a rule on the grounds of tiredness, real or feigned (as in Sally's attempt to get her way over the chocolate cake in example 9), or of distress. Pretend crying was used by several children in the second half of the third year (see example 24).

Excuses of intent. As adults we see as crucial the distinction between acts that were intended to harm others or to break rules of conduct and accidental acts with similar consequences (Darley and Zanna, 1982). Accidental acts are regarded as far less serious and are punished with much less severity in our legal system. We do not know at what stage children begin to make this distinction. Piaget wrote that there was "some reason to doubt whether a child of 6–7 could really distinguish an involuntary error from an intentional lie . . . the distinction is, at the best, in the process of formation" (1965, p. 145). In contrast, observations by Thomas Schulz (1980) suggest that in practice such a distinction may be made by children of three. Yet the children in our studies were rarely observed to use as an excuse that they "didn't mean to." The exceptions to this general finding, however, included some observations of children as young as 26 months.

19. Family J (Study 3). Child 26 months
Child climbs on M to investigate light switch.

M: You're hurting me!
C: Sorry. Sorry. Sorry. I don't mean to.

Later in the third year, children's references to intention were more clearly articulated. In the next example, Jay is resisting his mother's attempts to get him off the settee, where he is standing, with a reference to honorable intentions (cleaning the television set).

20. Family J (Study 3). Child 33 months

M: Get off!
C *(sits down):* Look. I'm not——(stands up). Mummy. I'm not——I'm not standing on there. I'm trying to get a paint off (rubs TV).
M: ——
C: I going try and get a paint off. All I'm trying to do is—— there.

The next example from an observation three months later shows Jay again reiterating his good intentions when in trouble. He was caught by his mother riding his tricycle over a toy train track, a forbidden action. He does it again, laughing, and draws her attention to his act.

C: You see that bit? (laughs).
M: (looks fierce).
C: I will. I will. I will. I'm trying to. I'm trying to, Ann! I'm trying to! (moves toys) I'm trying to——trying to. I'm trying to——trying to. I'm trying to.

While examples of such excuses are rare up to the age of 36 months, it is interesting to note that the excuse of the transgression's being made *in pretense* was occasionally made. In one observation of Kerry, a 30-month-old, and her brother, the two siblings were playing a wild and riotous pretend game in which their plastic paddling pool was upturned and serving as something else. When their mother angrily said that the pool "is not made for bouncing on" Kerry justified their actions by saying "we only making it up."

Justifications for transgression. Fig. 2.4 shows that during their third year the children with increasing frequency gave reasons for their prohibited actions. By far the most frequent justifications were those that referred to the child's own needs, wants, or feelings (Fig. 2.5). Other reasons were given too, but overwhelmingly it was the child's wants that are presented as

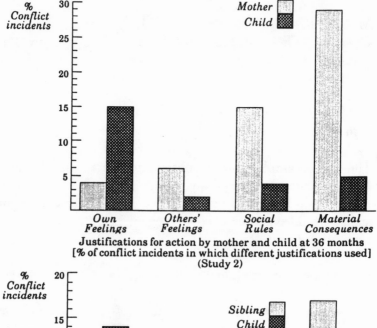

Justifications for action by mother and child at 36 months
[% of conflict incidents in which different justifications used]
(Study 2)

Justifications for action by sibling and child at 36 months
[% of conflict incidents in which different justifications used]
(Study 2)

Fig. 2.5 Justifications for action by child, mother, and sibling (Study 2)

why the mother should do *x* or the child should not do *y*. Next in frequency were excuses in terms of the material consequences of the child's or the other's action, and rules of sharing, turn-taking, or fairness. But their own welfare still was foremost.

Mothers, in comparison, referred more frequently to the feelings of other people as well as themselves, to social rules, and especially to the material consequences of the child's action. This emphasis on the consequences of the disputed action is worth noting. The propensity of young children to make moral judgments in terms of the consequences of the act, rather than the intentions of the actor, has been frequently noted and interpreted in terms of their immaturity. We might then see the emphasis of mothers on consequences as a sensitivity to the children's mode of thinking. We can also, however, see it as a feature of the children's actual experiences that in itself contributes to their way of judging actions. In daily life in the family, it is the consequences of their actions that most commonly lead to trouble for children.

Questioning the application of a rule. We have seen that children understood that rules apply differently to different people, citing babyhood and incapacity as excuses from family rules. But they also understood that rules did apply to other family members as well as to themselves, and they referred to this in confrontations with their mothers. They questioned why rules applied to them did not also apply to others.

21. *Family H (Study 2). Child 36 months*
M, sibling, and child in kitchen; M organizing cooking.

M: Would you two like to go and wash your hands? . . . Go and wash your hands, please.
C: Why don't you wash *your* hands?
M: Well, it's you two that are doing the cooking.

Children in the third year also began to make use of the excuse that other people, notably the parent or the observer, also performed the action prohibited by the mother. In the next example

Jay maintains (without any basis) that the observer (Penny) makes the same forbidden noise in drinking that he has just made.

22. Family J (Study 3). Child 33 months
Child is drinking noisily, filling mouth and saying "Aaaah!"

M: Stop it.
C: Penny do that. Len don't.
M: Penny wouldn't do that.

Direct questioning of rules escalates during the second half of the third year. That "Why?" questions begin to appear over these months has been clearly documented in studies of language acquisition. What is evident from our Cambridge studies is that, when these questions first appear, they are often directed at the mothers' attempts to control the children, suggesting that an important forum for the development of this crucial human capability—the ability to inquire of other people a cause or reason—is in the context of conflict over the child's own goals.

23. Family J (Study 3). Child 33 months
Child is in closet (previously forbidden).

M: Come on out now, please.
C: Why come out for?

In summary, children between two and three years old are, as moralists, able to comprehend the principles of harm to others, of responsibility for such harm, and of excuses from responsibility on the grounds of incapacity, involuntariness, or lack of intention. They understand that rules should apply to adults and to children, if not to babies, but that justifications on the grounds of personal welfare, social rules, and material consequences can be attempted. As psychologists too, they become notably more sophisticated in their own defense during this third year, as we see in the next section.

Understanding and further strategies

During the third year, children begin to use a whole set of new tactical moves when their wishes are frustrated, moves that reflect increasing understandings of family roles and relationships. They explicitly attempt to use other family relationships against their mothers. The next example is a continuation of the incident in example 20, in which Jay is resisting his mother's attempts to make him get off the settee.

> 24. *Family J (Study 3). Child 33 months*
>
> C: I'm not on the telly.
> M: Get *down*!!
> C: I'm not——(pretend cry). Mummy——off. I'll tell my Daddy come back home.
> M: Tell your Daddy.
> C: Hmm?
> M: I don't care.

Jay also tries to use what the observer Penny would like in his attempts to get his way:

> 25. *Same as above*
> Child is trying to climb on M's lap.
>
> C: I can't get up, Mum.
> M: I don't really want you.
> C: Please. Penny like me getting there. Help me up.

Other defensive moves made by the children during their third year are threats, bargains, and denial of *future* possible states as a reason for their mothers' prohibitions. Such negotiatory moves are, in the hands of a child only just three, not very refined psychological weapons. "I throw you in the bin," threatened Jay in a conflict with his mother at 36 months. More potentially powerful was his threat, cited above, to "tell my Daddy come back home." Denial of future consequences, again, was usually a simple denial. Impending rain was the reason Jay's mother gave him for not going outside, in an observation at 33 months. He countered this with, "It won't little bit rain," adding that he would take a towel out for his hair. Clumsy though such arguments are, they show us that even in their second year children do begin to take account of possible future states or moves by others.

The mother's part

The conversations during conflict with their mothers reveal not only an increasing articulateness on the children's part as they grow from 14 to 36 months old, but an increase in the frequency with which their mothers refer to social rules, to acceptable behavior, to the feelings of others, and to the consequences of the children's actions. Fig. 2.4 shows that to the 18-month-olds in Study 2 mothers gave reasons for their prohibitions in such terms in 33 percent of the incidents of conflict. To the same children at 24 months, the proportion of incidents in which such reasons were given rose to 51 percent, a highly significant increase (see Appendix Table 1). The mothers' expectations of what their children can understand, and how they can be expected to behave, change, and these changes parallel the developments in the children's own explicit use of social rules and feelings to justify actions and points of view. The growth in the children's cognitive ability to grasp what is expected behavior in the family is very clear: what the conversational analyses reveal is that the children are growing up in a world in which those rules are clearly and continually articulated for them, at a level that closely matches their own changing abilities. The significance of this discourse for a child's social understanding should not be underestimated.

Self-interest and the topic of conflict

One theme that stands out from these David-and-Goliath conflicts between very young children and their mothers is the children's growing understanding: of the feelings of the mother, of the connections between their own action and those maternal feelings, and of the "cherished classifications" of the family household. So far, incidents of conflict have been considered as if they were all alike. But mothers and young children confront one another over a tremendous range of issues: in British and American homes these can include whether it is acceptable to put toys down the toilet, pull the cat around by its tail, destroy a brother's castle of blocks, jump up and down on the sofa wearing muddy boots—or, to take the child's point of view, whether another piece of chocolate is required *now,* whether help with a toy or a cuddle is needed absolutely this minute, or conversely whether adult attempts to provide help in getting dressed or setting up a game are an outrage. Not only does the focus of the dispute vary greatly in nature—from attempts to get a child to behave "nicely" to attempts to stop a child from hurting someone—but the intensity of emotion expressed by the antagonists varies widely. There can be, as we have seen, loud anger or relative calm on both sides, or amusement on one side and irritation or anger on the other.

A closer look at our mothers and children in conflict begins to show us which issues are most salient to the children and illuminates the question of what kinds of distinctions the children make between transgressions of different sorts. How does the topic of the dispute affect the children's behavior? Over which topics do the children produce their most mature strategies of argument and which are they most angry about?

At each of the ages observed for children in Study 2 (18, 24, and 36 months), the two most common topics of conflict between child and mother were destructive, wild behavior (26 percent of conflicts on average) and breaches of family routines (referred to from now on as "convention" conflicts), which accounted for about 25 percent of conflicts. At 24 months there was a sudden increase in conflict over caretaking—arguments about toilet training, cleanliness, being dressed, and so on. These doubled in frequency between 18 and 24 months but were less prominent in the arguments at 36 months. But arguments over "rights"—possession, sharing, turns, fairness—were also common, at each age. They accounted for about 20 percent of conflicts. Finally, at roughly similar frequencies there were conflicts over manners ("Say ta" . . . "No!"), over hurting or unkindness, and over invasion of physical space (standing deliberately so close to someone's newspaper that they are unable to read it, being a nuisance by following too close, and so on). Each of these accounted for 5–8 percent of conflict incidents.

The topic of the conflict dramatically affected the children's behavior. First, they were much more angry and distressed in conflicts over their rights than over other issues at 18 months (Appendix Table 1). In 24 percent of such incidents they expressed anger or distress, while in only 9 percent of conflict incidents over other issues were they upset in this way. By 24 months, both these conflicts over rights and conventions aroused distress and anger more than other topics. Interestingly, neither conflict over destruction nor conflict over aggression was likely to cause distress or anger: rather, these were much more likely to make the child laugh. The association between incidents in which the child was reprimanded for hurting another—the most clearly moral issue—and the child's hilarity is particularly striking. Thus disputes over the children's own rights caused considerable distress and anger, especially at 18 months; issues of decision over more conventional routines within the family were also a matter that aroused such emotion. In contrast, the arguments over wild behavior and physical aggression were a source of mirth.

It was not only the children's emotional displays that differed with conflict over different issues. What they said—whether they attempted to justify or excuse themselves, deny, blame, conciliate, or simply stop the mother—also differed according to the topic of dispute. The pattern of these differences in the children's justifications complements in an interesting way the differences in their emotional behavior. Fig. 2.6 shows that it was those issues over which the children at 18 months were most distressed or angry that at 36 months they were most

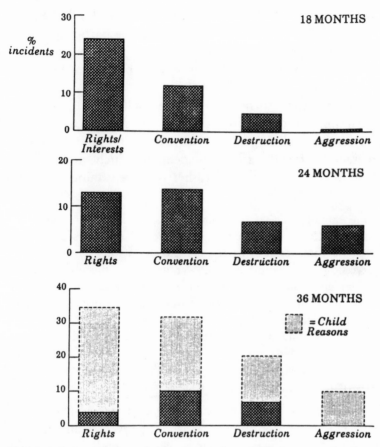

Fig. 2.6 Anger/distress shown in mother-child disputes (Study 2)

likely to justify. In 35 percent of disputes over rights, they produced justifications, as compared with only 15 percent of the disputes over destruction and aggression. The children, that is, marshaled their most mature behavior over those issues that earlier their emotional behavior had suggested they *cared* most about. In contrast, in the disputes over the issues at which they had laughed in the earlier visits (destruction, boisterous behavior, aggression), they were significantly less likely to offer reasons as three-year-olds. And in the emotionally neutral discussions between child and mother—discussions about what was the case rather than about how someone should behave—when one might suppose that they would be particularly prone to reason calmly, the 36-month-old children produced justifications for their propositions in only 20 percent of the discussions.

It is interesting to note that James Sully (1896) comments several times that children often show their most advanced behavior when their goals are frustrated and their self-interest threatened. After describing incidents in which the child C attempts to get his way with rather poor reasoning during the third year, Sully remarks:

> One cannot say that these first incursions into the domain of logic do Master C. particular credit. Perhaps we may see later on that he came to use his rational faculty with more skill and precision and to turn it to nobler uses than the invention of subterfuges whereby he might get his wilful way . . . As might be expected from his general use of subterfuge about this time, he showed a lamentable want of moral responsibility. Thus (at 31 months) he was noticed by his mother putting a spill of paper over the fireguard into the fire so as to light it. His mother at once said: "Ningi mustn't do that." Whereupon he impudently retorted: "Ningi not doing that, paper doing it." (p. 449)

What inferences can we draw from the pattern of associations between topic, emotion, and reasoning revealed in the Cambridge study? One is that children use their intelligence on what matters to them emotionally. Another, not incompatible with the first, is that the experience of distress and anger during these particular conflicts may actually contribute to their learning—that the arousal they experience heightens their vigilance and attentive powers.

A third possibility is that the mother's behavior during these particular conflicts is an important influence. If mothers consistently used reasoning techniques in conflicts over particular issues and not in others, it could be that the children learn similar strategies from them. Mothers are indeed more likely to reason with children in conflicts in which the younger child is distressed or angry than in incidents in which the child is not upset. And they are more likely to use reasoning in conflicts over rights than in other conflicts, at both 24 and 36 months (Appendix Table 1).

There is a fourth possible interpretation for this pattern of children's reasoning at three years old: children use reasoning only when they believe reasoning is a practical strategy. That is, they do not use reasoning in disputes over aggression or boisterous behavior because they know that reasoning won't get them out of that kind of scrape.

The arguments between very young children and their mothers do, then, have serious implications for our ideas on the development of social and moral understanding. We see that children even in their second year are intensely interested in social rules and in the transgression of such rules; that they marshal considerable powers of understanding in confrontation with their mothers over the rules; that the increase in their powers is paralleled by a change in the emotions they express; that there are marked differences in behavior in relation to different kinds of cultural breach; that they grow up in a world of discourse about social rules. The rules for which they show concern, moreover, are not solely the idiosyncratic or local habits of one particular family, but rather rules that are part of a much wider cultural context. Respect for possession rights and avoidance of injury to another are very general principles in our culture; the significance of incapacity, ill health, or lack of intention in relation to transgression is central to our society's notions of what is permissible. The wider cultural concepts of morality are already part of our children's framework for understanding their world. And already the cherished classifications of middle- and working-class western life are a source of interest—sufficiently well understood to be a source of teasing and humor.

How do these changes in understanding and emotion relate to the child's developing sense of self and other? How should we conceptualize the relation between affective and cognitive changes in children? Can close observation illuminate the current disagreements and controversies about the development of moral understanding? Before examining these questions, let us first turn from one set of family disputes to two others: from the David-and-Goliath disputes between child and parent to the Cain-and-Abel disputes between child and sibling, and to the child as witness to other family disputes.

3

Confronting the Sibling

The weakness then of infant limbs, not its will, is its innocence.
Myself have seen and known even a baby envious; it could not
speak, yet it turned pale and looked bitterly on its foster-
brother. Who knows not this? . . . Is that too innocence, when
the fountain of milk is flowing in rich abundance, not to en-
dure one to share it, though in extremest need, and whose very
life yet depends thereon?

—St. Augustine, *Confessions*, c. 397–400

The power of jealousy between siblings is a theme running throughout mythology, literature, and history—an emotion seen by Freud and writers before and after him as having
lifelong effects on an individual's personality. We can question
the precise scientific basis for such a claim, but we cannot doubt
the emotional urgency of the uninhibited rage that young siblings can show toward one another. Such anger often leaves a
lasting trace—even from the second year, as Thomas Carlyle
comments in his reminiscences of 1881:

> My earliest memory of all is a mad passion of rage at my elder
> brother John . . . in which my Father too figures though dimly,
> as a kind of cheerful comforter and soother. I had broken my
> little brown stool, by madly throwing it at my brother; and felt
> for the first time, the united pangs of Loss and Remorse. I was
> perhaps hardly more than 2 years old . . . though all is quite
> legible for myself. (quoted in Sampson and Sampson, 1985)

The lamentations of parents observing the violence between
their children echo down the centuries; the behavior described
and the distress felt by parents are strikingly similar whether the
witness is from the tenth, eighteenth, or twentieth century. Although the actions of a jealous brother or sister are undoubtedly

upsetting to witness (let alone to receive), they are also extremely revealing. If we look closely at the exchanges between young siblings, we gain an illuminating perspective on the nature of the child's growing understanding of the feelings and needs of another person, and of the social and moral rules within the family. It is a picture that in some ways differs from that revealed in the disputes between child and parent, but the developmental changes are similar.

One obvious difference between the sibling-child and the mother-child disputes concerns the interests of the children, which are far closer than those between child and adult. This matching of interests means that two children are very likely to compete for similar goods; the interests of the child are frequently directly threatened by the sibling. It also means that each child knows well what the other particularly likes and dislikes, especially if they are close in age. What pleases a three-year-old is not very different from what pleases his five-year-old brother. This closeness of interests, and the familiarity of children who share daily intimacy, means that young children probably have less difficulty in understanding how to annoy, comfort, or anticipate the moods and responses of their siblings than those of their parents. The accuracy with which children read the expressions and wishes of other children who are in some sense competitors was commented on by Maria Edgeworth in the eighteenth century, in no-nonsense terms. She firmly linked the ability directly to the children's powers of "reason" and the strength of competition between them:

> Two hungry children, with their eager eyes fixed on one and the same bason of milk, do not sympathise with each other, though they have the same sensations; each perceives that if the other eats the bread and milk, he cannot eat it . . . We may observe, that the more quickly children reason, the sooner they discover how far their interests are any ways incompatible with the interests of their companions . . . Children, who are accurate observers of the countenance, and who have a superior degree of penetration, discover very early the symptoms of displeasure, or

of affection, in their friends; they also perceive quickly the dangers of rivalship from their companions. (1798, p. 275)

This competitive similarity of interests, coupled with the child's grasp of what upsets and excites the sibling *and* the uninhibited nature of the sibling relationship, means that sibling quarrels are more often emotionally loaded than are most disputes with the mother. On average, the children in the forty families of our Study 2 expressed intense anger or distress in 28 percent and 21 percent of the incidents of sibling conflict at 24 and 36 months respectively. In contrast, the proportions of mother-child disputes in which the child showed such distress or anger were 10 percent and 9 percent at the same ages.

Signs of new understanding

There are some important parallels between a child's behavior in conflict with a parent and with a sibling: these concern developmental changes in emotion and understanding. The children expressed intense anger and distress during sibling conflicts with increasing frequency during the first half of the second year, just as they did in disputes with the mother, differences that were significant between 14 and 18 months (see Fig. 3.1 for changes in physical aggression over this period). They also displayed increasing powers of understanding, as shown by their ability to provoke a sibling by teasing.

Teasing

During the second year, teasing became both more frequent and more elaborate. At 16 and 18 months, the teasing incidents we observed included the following behavior: removing the sibling's comfort object in the course of a fight; leaving a fight in order to go and destroy a cherished possession of the sibling; holding a cherished object just out of reach of the sibling; pulling the sibling's thumb (sucked in moments of stress) out of his mouth; pushing a toy spider at a sibling who was reportedly afraid of spiders. By the end of the second year, such acts,

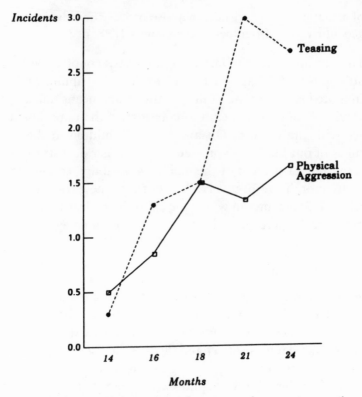

Fig. 3.1 Changes in frequency of teasing and aggression to sibling in second year (Study 1)

observed in each of the children in Study 1, had become more elaborate. One child whose sibling had three imaginary friends, named Lily, Allelujah, and Peepee, taunted the sibling by announcing that *she* was the imaginary friend. It was an act that reliably angered the sibling, and an act of considerable intellectual virtuosity for a child of 24 months.

The interest of these actions lies in the understanding they reflect of what will upset or annoy a particular person. Teasing of the mother was also, as we have seen, quite common ("I don't love you, Mummy" was a technique already developed at 24 months by two of the children in the six families in Study 1). Yet it did not reach the frequency or the elaboration of the teasing of the sibling, a difference that might well reflect the relative difficulty that the child faced in understanding what can upset an adult as opposed to another child, as well as the greater emotional urgency of exchanges with the sibling. Teasing of the sibling remained frequent throughout the third year and was as commonly shown by younger as by older siblings. So the ability to understand what will upset the other child develops very early, and the motivation to act in this way does not decrease over the preschool years. Of the forty secondborn children in Study 2, seventeen were observed to tease by 18 months, and thirty-six by 24 months.

Enlisting adult help

The children's behavior during sibling conflicts reflected not only their understanding of what would annoy a sibling but also their growing grasp of what was sanctioned behavior within the family. This was evident in their attempts to enlist adult help. The world of adult values and rules is very much part of the context of sibling disputes in the home, and children learn quickly how to enlist adult aid or to avoid adult sanctions in disputes with siblings. There was, for example, a striking difference in the probability of appealing for help, depending on the initiator of the physical aggression or teasing. In Study 1, we found that in 66 percent of the incidents in which the sibling behaved aggressively, the children appealed to their mothers for help. In contrast, they appealed to their mothers in only 3 percent of incidents in which they *themselves* had acted in this way—a dramatic difference (Appendix Table 3). In itself, such anticipation of the behavior of the parent does not require elaborate understanding; a pet dog faced with an owner's disapproval might well behave in the same way. But the differences in the children's attempts to enlist parental aid in the face of their own or another's transgression do demonstrate a growing comprehension of what is sanctioned behavior. It also demonstrates that children use such understanding when their own interests are threatened.

The earliest appeals to the mother that we observed in our Cambridge children were nonverbal. The 14- and 16-month-olds acted in the following ways during conflicts with siblings: the child looks at the mother while pointing at the sibling and vocalizing or crying; the child runs over to the mother and pulls her toward the sibling; the child shows her a wound inflicted by the sibling and gestures toward the sibling. Over the months that followed, the children became increasingly articulate in their appeals. In both their direct protests to the sibling and in their appeals to the mother, the developments in understanding are like those observed in the mother-child disputes, as their conversations reveal.

Conversations about rules

The idea of responsibility. The children were often explicit about the connection between actions and pain caused by actions. In Example 14 in the last chapter, the child connected her own action and the pain caused to the sibling; in the example here the connection is between the sibling's action and the child's pain:

1. *Family N (Study 1). Child 21 months*
Child is crying, comes to M.

M (sympathetically): What's the matter?
C: Annie banged me. Hurt.

By the third year, the children's threats to hurt their siblings made their understanding of agency all too clear. In the next example, Jay at 28 months attempts to "sort out" his older brother, with his father's encouragement; as he gets the worst of the fight, he uses the excuse of a headache to abandon the attempt and indeed complains that his brother has hurt *him*.

2. *Family J (Study 3). Child 28 months*
Sibling (Len) and child are in conflict.

Father to C: Sort him out.
Sib: Oh no!

C: Len (hits him).

Sib: Oh no!

C: Biff him now (hits him). (To M) Hitting it. Mum look. Do Len fight. Enough. Got headache (takes gloves off) . . . Len hurt me. Len hurt me. He biff me.

Discussion of responsibility—in this case, always the sibling's—appeared toward the end of the second year, as we saw in the previous chapter. The children also began to deny their actions and to blame their siblings during the third year; such behavior frequently followed similar claims by the older sibling.

A principle of justice?

Justifications and excuses. The children were just as likely to use reasons in disputes with their siblings as with their mothers, at both 24 and 36 months (Fig. 3.2). And the nature of those justifications is similar. The only significant difference was that at 24 months the children were more likely to refer to social rules in disputes with siblings than with mothers (Appendix Table 3). Here the rule in question was usually possession, an issue at the center of many conflicts. By 36 months, the patterns of justification made to sibling and to mother were much alike, as was the proportion of conflict incidents that included justification—increasing from 18 percent (24 months) to 28 percent at 36 months.

As in the mother-child disputes, it was the child's own wishes, feelings, or needs that were most frequently referred to: in 14 percent of disputes with siblings at 36 months, the children's protests referred to their own feelings. Next most common were references to social rules—primarily rules of possession, sharing, or turns—and to the material consequences of the sibling's actions (6 percent and 5 percent of sibling disputes, respectively). In the next example, the older sister runs for comfort to her mother after a fight with her brother; the mother's cup of tea wobbles in the saucer as she rushes past, and the younger brother draws attention to this in an attempt to get at his sister.

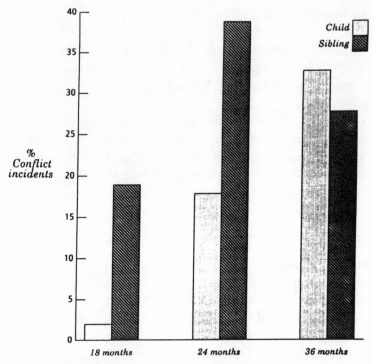

Fig. 3.2 Proportion of conflict incidents in which child and sibling reason/justify their actions (Study 2)

3. Family M (Study 3). Child 30 months
Child and sibling hit each other.

C: That hurts. (Sibling runs to M; M's cup wobbles in saucer.) Don't. You'll hurt Mummy tea.

Some of the justifications in terms of rules were not applied with great skill and often involved simple variants on the rules articulated by the older sibling.

4. Family C (Study 2). Child 36 months
Sibling requests turn on bouncing ball.

Sib: Can I have a go? Can I do that? May I?
C: When I've had two goes.

Sib: Yes, it's your turn so . . . so you have two goes. And I'm four so I have four, have four goes. Yes! I have four goes. (A few minutes later C tries to get ball back.)
Sib: No! I have four goes. Four goes. Four. (C gets ball back, sib again requests turn.)
Sib: Can I have a go?
C: No. When I've had eight goes. 'Cos I'm . . .

It is interesting that, although the children were far more likely at 36 months to articulate reasons why the siblings should change their behavior than they had been at 24 months, the sophistication of those reasons was not usually striking or notably different from that of the 24-month justifications. Appeals to the sibling at both ages were primarily in terms of the child's own wants or rights of possession.

Questioning a rule. Just as the children showed some notion of the symmetry with which rules could be applied to others as well as themselves in disputes with the mother (see example 21, Chapter 2), so too the children indicated that rules applied to them should also be applied to the sibling. In the next example, John angrily points out that his sister Annie is still doing what he has been told not to do.

5. Family N (Study 1). Child 21 months
Both children have pushed stools up to kitchen counter
next to oven, to investigate cooking materials.

M to C: Ah ah! Don't touch please. Hot! (removes child).
C: (protest noise).
M: Oh I know!
C (angrily): Annie going there!
M to sib: Annie come right away. Right away.

The same child, who at this stage is very hostile to his older sister, does not simply refuse to comply with commands from his mother but suggests that Annie should carry out the disliked chores.

6. *Same as above*
M is trying to get child to put away train set.

M: Can you put the train back in the cupboard?
C: No. Annie. Annie.
M: Well, Annie didn't get it out, did she?

John's hostility to his sister is also reflected in his attempts to prevent his mother from giving his sister the objects she needed for her play. In the next example, the siblings are quarreling over who should have some blocks; Annie the sibling was building with them, and John took some away. Their mother intervenes by prohibiting the fight and distributing the blocks equally.

7. *Same as above*

M: Hey, hey, no fighting! (gives equal numbers of blocks to C and sib).
C: Not Annie. Not that (throws away his own blocks).
M: You don't want that? Can Annie have all of them?
C: No.
M: Annie can't have them, but you don't want them?
C: No! No!

In case the interpretation of this exchange appears doubtful, let me note that several other similar exchanges occurred during the observations of this child at 21 months. For instance, when his mother offered his sister a drink, John intervened to say that Annie should not be given one, even though he did not himself want one.

8. *Same as above*

M to sib: Annie, do you want a drink?
C to M: Not Annie get drink.
M to C: If Annie wants a drink, she can have a drink.
C to M: No!

M to C: Do *you* want a drink?
C to M: No!

Although not yet two years old, John is attempting to intervene in the interaction between his mother and sister, to his sister's disadvantage. Of course, much younger children attempt to disrupt affectionate exchanges between their parents and siblings (or indeed between their parents, as reported by Cummings, Zahn-Waxler, and Radke-Yarrow, 1981) through physical intervention. What is notable about these examples is that they are verbal, making it clear that the child is monitoring with some vigilance the verbal exchange between other family members.

The understanding that rules of positive justice can be used with reference to the rights of other people, yet also in the interests of self, was apparent in the third year. In the next example, Martin attempts to keep his older sister Chrissie from joining the game of soccer he is playing with his mother, by insisting that she is taking their mother's turn.

9. Family C (Study 2). Child 36 months
Child and M are playing with ball. Sibling attempts to join game by kicking ball when it comes near her.

C to sib: No! It's Mummy's go again. No! It was Mummy's go again.
M to C: Chrissie did it for me.
C: I'll put this ball away. I'm going to put it away if Chrissie's going to spoil it for Mummy.

Incidents of quarrels between siblings in which the children drew their mother's attention to the sibling's transgressions became increasingly common during the third year. In the next example, the mother in fact reprimands the older sibling for telling tales on the child, who then proceeds to claim that the sibling had transgressed in three different ways: by telling tales, by touching the newly baked cakes, and by frowning—an action that she herself has just been scolded for. The insistence that the older sibling should be punished rather than the child is typical of children of this age period.

10. Family M (Study 3). Child 30 months

Sib to M: Mick touched . . . He took those four.
M to sib: Don't tell tales.
Sib to M: I'm not.
C to Sib: Am.
Sib: (pokes C, who protests).
M to both: Gonna argue, you can get down.
C to M: Janie——Janie get down, Mummy.
M to C: Yes. And you will too if you keep on arguing.
C to M: No Janie. Not me.
Sib to C: You will.
M to both: I shall make you both get down if you argue.
C to M: No. Janie. Not me. (Several turns later, C draws attention to sib touching cakes.)
C to M: Mummy. Look. Look. Janie din it. (Later M reprimands C for frowning at her.)
C to M: Janie frown.

Examples of the younger sibling drawing the mother's attention to misdeeds of the older occur in the observations of every child that we studied during the third year. Typical is an observation of Annie, who reports to her mother on a succession of transgressions by her older sister Carol.

11. Family A (Study 3). Child 30 months
Siblings and M are in garden. C and sibling are playing with hose, paddling pool, and water.

C: Mummy.
M: Yes?
C: Carol got it soaking wet . . .
C: Mum.
M: Yes?

C: Carol's——Carol's touching a sprayer.
M: Is she? (goes to look). She's not doing anything.
C: She not doing it now! . . .
C: Carol's getting it all over my hair.

Differentiation of claim according to person. Although the general pattern of the children's verbal protests and justifications was similar in conflict with the sibling and with the mother, it was noticeable that the most advanced arguments or claims were made to the mother rather than to the sibling. A particularly striking example was the following exchange.

12. Family S (Study 2). Child 36 months
Sibling (David) and C (Megan) in dispute over who can play with toy vacuum cleaner. It belongs to Megan, but David has just managed to repair it. He plays with it, she attempts to get it back.

Sib to M: I wanted to do it. Because I fixed it up. And made it work.
M to Sib: Well, you'll have to wait your turn.
Sib to M: ——switched.
M to C: Are you going to let David have a turn?
C to M: I have to do it. *Ladies* do it.
M to C: Yes, ladies do it. Yes, and men do it sometimes. Daddy sometimes does the hoovering, doesn't he?
C to M: But I do it sometimes.
M to C: Yes, but Daddy does it sometimes so you let David do it.

Under the urgent pressure of her concern to get her toy back from her brother, 36-month-old Megan makes a claim to their mother about gender role differences, behavior of remarkable maturity for such a young child. Her older brother also makes his claim to the mother rather than to his sister. Both siblings behave as if reasoned justification of any elaboration made to a sibling is not a useful strategy, but is appropriately made to the mother. The children's differential behavior to mother and sibling reflects the growing subtlety of their social knowledge.

What is clear from these observations is that children from 18 months on have some grasp of how to affect the feeling state of a sibling; they know well what particular objects or activities have a special significance for the sibling. Strikingly similar observations of understanding in the context of sibling conflict have been reported in the work of Sara Harkness and Charles Super (1985) on the Kipsigis in Kenya; incidents are cited in which two-year-olds deny their own responsibility, blame the sibling, and draw the mother's attention to the misdeeds of the sibling.

In the encounters among our Cambridge siblings, we also see the beginnings of an understanding of certain rules of positive justice, a practical grasp of how such rules can be used when one's interests are threatened. For it is, I would emphasise, under the stress of situations in which the children's own interests are impeded that they demonstrate their comprehension of what will upset their sibling and of how their mothers can be enlisted as support. In these conflicts between peers, effective argument depends on some grasp of the other's goals and rights. As Ann Eisenberg and Catherine Garvey (1981) show in their analysis of arguments between peers of three years and above, "sociological thought begins to develop under the impetus of the clash and conflicts of child-child interactions." These older children "seemed to know that partners expected a reason for disagreement or noncompliance . . . An opposition must be accompanied by a reason. To get his own way in the interaction, the child must recognize the rights and intentions of the other individual." We turn next to family exchanges in which the child's own interests are not so directly threatened, incidents in which the children's mothers and siblings are in dispute. How do the children respond to transgressions by another in which they are not directly involved?

Witnessing disputes

"It is a matter of astonishment to me, to see discreet and good people universally overrun with the false notion, that children do not observe, as if because they are children they neither hear, nor see, nor feel" (Nelson, 1753, p. 184). This point is one that is noted by many of the early observers of children. Albertine de Saussure comments with respect to one-year-olds: "At this age an intelligent child will read the expression of our feelings and countenance: we may see reflected on his little face every shade of our own humour: he knows not whence these changes in our disposition arise, but he partakes in them, and though ignorant of the cause, sympathises in the effect" (1828–1832, p. 86).

The most systematic information that we have on the development of children's responses to family disputes during this period of transition from infancy to childhood comes from the studies by Cummings, Zahn-Waxler, Radke-Yarrow, and their colleagues of children between ten months and two and a half years (1981, 1984). They asked mothers to record the behavior of their children following incidents in which family members displayed anger. The results showed that, by about one year, children were not only aware of others' angry interactions but often responded with distress or anger. Pleasure and altruistic responses were rare. The same group of researchers also made experimental studies that demonstrate again that witnessing angry interchanges between others has a powerful effect on young children: when children playing in a laboratory playroom overheard two strangers arguing in an adjacent room, the children commonly stopped playing and subsequently behaved toward one another with significantly more aggression (Cummings, Iannotti, and Zahn-Waxler, 1985).

In our Cambridge studies we systematically examined the children's behavior when arguments took place between their mother and sibling. Some 297 disputes of this sort were recorded when the children were 18 and 24 months old (their siblings were on average 45 and 50 months old at the two time points). These disputes were of considerable interest to the secondborn children: they rarely ignored the arguments but responded to 72 percent of them at 18 months, and to 78 percent at 24 months. What happened between these two other people was highly salient to the children. The *way* that they responded varied. In some incidents the children simply watched, soberly. In others they imitated the sibling's prohibited action or laughed; sometimes they attempted to punish the sibling; and sometimes they attempted to support one or other of the antagonists. These supportive responses were particularly interesting since they were innovative actions, not merely repetitions of the behavior of mother or sibling. They clearly demonstrated that the children understood what it was that the combatants wanted.

13. Family D (Study 1). Child 21 months
Dispute between sibling and M about whether sibling
can play with noisy toy musical instruments. C runs to
toy cupboard, finds drum, brings it to sibling.

The children's verbal comments during such conflict incidents were also interesting. Sometimes the children made judgmental comments on the behavior of the sibling.

14. Family D (Study 1). Child 24 months
Sibling shows M that she has drawn on piece of jigsaw
puzzle.

Sib to M: Look.
M to sib: You aren't supposed to draw on them, Clare. You
    should know better. You only draw on pieces of paper.
    You don't draw on puzzles.
Sib to M: Why?
M to sib: Because they aren't pieces of paper.
C: Naughty.
M: Yes, that is a naughty thing to do.

In the next example, the social knowledge of Jan (in fact very fond of her older brother Tim), is expressed both in action and in her comments.

15. Family L (Study 2). Child 24 months
M and Tim are arguing over whether he has eaten M's
cookie. Dispute continues over 5 speaker turns. C picks
up block and throws it at sib, hitting him on forehead.

M: Jan! Why did you do that?
C: ——cry.
M: What do you say to Tim? What do you say to him? Why
did you smack him?
C: Bad boy.
M: Because he's been a bad boy?
C: Yes.

The motivation for Jan's action is not entirely clear. She might
have been concerned that her brother had upset their mother and
wished to punish him, on her mother's behalf. It is possible that
she was angry with her brother for other reasons and used this
opportunity to express her hostility. Or perhaps she wanted to
draw attention to herself and to interrupt the exchange between
her brother and mother. But although we cannot be certain about
the motivation for her action, we can see that she is able to use
terms of moral judgment. Already by 24 months she understands
something of the rules about acceptable behavior within the
family and uses this understanding in the context of her family
relationships, to explain her behavior to her mother. The next
example is a similar incident, in which 26-month-old Polly passes
judgment on who is at fault in a dispute between her older sister
Helen and their mother. The motivation again is open to question, but the moral judgment is quite "appropriate."

16. Family C (Study 3). Child 26 months
M and sibling are arguing over whether TV should be
turned off.

M to sib: Switch it off.
Sib to M: I don't want you to switch it off! No! (repeated 8
times).

C to sib: No!
Sib to M: No (repeated 5 times). Naughty Mummy!
M to sib: Hey. Come on.
Sib to M: No (repeated 3 times).
C to sib (holding M): Not naughty. Naughty Helen (hits sib).

Sensitivity to emotion or to topic?

What were the children responding to in the disputes between their mothers and siblings? It could be that what interested them was the emotion expressed by the antagonists; or perhaps the children were interested in the topic of the dispute. One way of examining this is to look at how the children responded to mother-sibling disputes on different topics. Our results show that the children did indeed behave differently in response to different kinds of argument (Appendix Table 3). When the sibling behaved aggressively, the children were more likely to censure or punish the sibling than in incidents where the topic of dispute was a transgression of some social rule over possession of objects or other "conventional" acceptable behavior. Here the children usually laughed or imitated the sibling. They generally ignored arguments between mother and sibling that were power disputes, in which one antagonist was refusing the request of the other. These differences in the salience of disputes focused on different topics were evident even in those arguments in which no emotion was expressed.

The topic itself was important to the children, then, not solely the emotion expressed by the antagonists. But, in practice, topic and emotion are closely connected. In arguments about aggressive behavior or pain caused by the sibling, mother and sibling were more likely to be angry or distressed than in incidents where the dispute was simply about, say, where the sibling should leave his coat. So it is still possible that the differences in the children's responses to different topics of conflict were responses to the varying emotions that the mother and sibling were expressing.

Fig. 3.3 shows that the children were indeed sensitive to the emotion expressed by the pair in confrontation (see also Appendix Table 4). The most common responses to incidents in which anger or distress was expressed by either mother or sibling were that the child watched or attempted to support one of the participants; the children rarely laughed in such incidents. In contrast, when their siblings laughed in certain situations, the children also laughed or imitated the sibling's action; rarely did they support either the sibling or mother. Thus the children's responses were

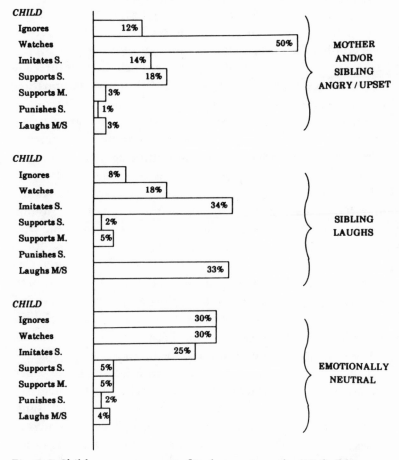

Fig. 3.3 Child responses to conflict between mother and sibling, according to emotion of combatants (Study 2)

in some respects appropriate to the emotions expressed by the other family members. To a distressed sibling, they offered support. To a laughing sibling, they responded by laughing themselves.

The results from the observations at 18 and at 24 months suggest that children of these ages are responsive to both the emotion and the topic of dispute between other family members. What the young child witnesses, and responds to, is an event in which two important features are combined: a transgression of a rule explicitly discussed and a display of emotion by two people with whom the child has a close and complex relationship.

By the time the children were three years old, there were far fewer conflicts between their older siblings (now aged on average 5 years) and their mothers. Family life with children of three and five years is much calmer than life with children of one and three. Because we recorded only 68 incidents of mother-sibling conflict, a detailed analysis of the children's responses is inappropriate. But at least we can note which conflicts they showed interest in and which they ignored. By the 36-month stage, the topic of the argument was clearly of importance in accounting for differences in the children's response to the dispute. There was, however, a notable difference in the salience of the topic of the sibling's dispute with the mother and the salience of the same topic when it was the focus of the child's own dispute with the mother. Recall the anger, distress, and reasoning shown when the children were confronting their mothers over an issue of rights. This was the topic that at 18 months roused the most anger and distress and, by 36 months, produced the most reasons. In contrast, children were most likely to ignore disputes between sibling and mother over rights (those of the sibling and the mother). In 73 percent of such incidents, the children showed no interest. An argument about someone else's rights was of much less interest to them than an argument about boisterous behavior, destruction, or disgusting (to the mother) actions—they showed interest in 76 percent of these disputes. They were often amused by such incidents and frequently laughed or imitated the sibling's forbidden action, as they had done at 24 months. They also sometimes made comments to the mother about their own good behavior and the bad consequences that were likely to result for the sibling. In a typical incident, the mother told her older son to stop shouting and, when he refused to comply, threatened that Father Christmas would bring him no toys this year if he continued. His 36-month-old sibling promptly said to their mother, "Me not shouting." A few moments later the older boy, frustrated at his failure over a jigsaw, again screamed and was briefly censured by his mother. The three-year-old commented, "Father Christmas don't get Tommy any toys, Mummy."

The question of how far the children were interested in the emotional behavior of the antagonists as opposed to the topic of dispute remains unclear. In general the children were not more likely to attend to those incidents in which intense negative emotions were expressed. Yet none of the incidents in which destruction was the topic, *and* the combatants expressed intense emotion, was ignored; and only 25 percent of incidents in which the sibling laughed were ignored. The important real-life link between the topic of dispute and the emotions expressed by participants is again evident.

In the observations of children whose interests are challenged by the competing interests of a sibling, we see developments in behavior and in discussion of rules that parallel those revealed in the mother-child disputes. As witnesses to arguments between their siblings and mothers, the children show a sensitivity to both the topic of the dispute and the interests of the antagonists— hardly egocentric behavior in the classical sense. The rules they use and discuss are, as in the disputes with their mothers, not just the particular practices of their families but the general moral tenets of the wider social world. The principal of positive justice (sharing, equal distribution of goods) and the importance of application of rules to both sibling and self are dominating themes in disputes with siblings. And the practices of society with respect to gender are already becoming part of the children's views of how things are ordered, well enough understood to be used as a weapon in a fast-expanding armory of justification.

4

Understanding, Self-Interest, and Family Relationships

In this chapter two general developmental issues are considered in the light of these observations: first, the nature of children's understanding of others and of social rules; second, the importance of self-interest, social relationships, and emotional experience in the development of this understanding.

The nature of social understanding

The observations of children in conflict with their mothers and siblings, and as witnesses of conflict, show that children during the second and third year have some practical understanding of others' feelings and intentions. Their grasp is a practical one in the sense that it is used to annoy, comfort, or support. To use a term such as "practical" should make it clear that I do not, at least for children during their second year, assume that children of this age are reflecting upon others' feelings in any elaborate way. It is still a partial understanding, intuitive rather than reflective (see Shweder, Turiel, and Much, 1981). But the observations of teasing and of support offered to those who are distressed or frustrated also make it clear that, in the context of disputes in which the child's goals are of central importance or those in which family members are in conflict, children do understand the connection between their own actions and the other person's state of pain, anger, or amusement. And the children's powers of understanding are commonly used in struggles to gain their own way. (William James's notion of knowledge of acquaintance, as opposed to knowledge-about [1890, p. 221], and

M.J. Packer's notion, from Heidegger, of an understanding that is "ready-to-hand" [1986] capture a similar sense of a knowledge that does not entail reflection.)

Observations of conflict also highlight the children's interest in and growing understanding of social rules, adult standards, and the nature of power relationships within the family. Jerome Kagan (1981) has documented this awareness of adult standards in an experimental setting for children of 19 months and older. What is particularly striking here is that the children are not simply increasingly aware of what is approved or expected behavior. Rather, they are beginning to grasp what William Damon has argued is the essence of social knowledge: the nature of the relations between people and the transactions that regulate those relations. "A child experiences, and makes sense out of society, only by gaining knowledge of such social relations as authority, attachment, and friendship, and of such social transactions as punishment, sharing, kindness, and hostility" (Damon, 1977, p. 2). On the issue of authority, Damon emphasizes that children do not try systematically to learn all the demands and rules of their world and that, even if they could, it would do them little good. The understanding of authority involves much more than a catalogue of rules. The child has to understand the basis for why one obeys, who one obeys when, who and when one can disobey, who and when one can expect to command, and so on: "Authority like all other important social concepts, is best understood as a subjective, dynamic relation between persons" (p. 3).

It is the child's practical grasp of how authority relations within the family can be used that is so striking in these early years. By two years old, children are using maternal authority for support in their fights with siblings; they draw their mother's attention to the siblings' misdemeanors, while pointing out that they themselves have not acted in the same way. Early in the second year, they distinguish between occasions when they can expect to enlist maternal authority for their support and when they cannot. As we saw, one child of three in conflict with his mother threatened to call his father for support. To suggest that such young children understand the subtlety of authority relations may seem a farfetched claim, but it is one that is supported by some observations of children from a very different culture, in the Solomon Islands. Infants and toddlers there spend long periods in the care of older siblings, who are carefully instructed in child care. Karen Watson-Gegeo (in a personal communication) notes that, at 18 months, a child who is looked after by a three-to-four-year-old sibling will, while the sibling is in charge, obey the sibling's commands. However, when the mother is present and the sibling is no longer in the authority role, the 18-month-olds often disregard the sibling's orders.

Studies of children's use of language have made a similar point. Susan Ervin-Tripp, discussing the child's understanding of the different ways in which people can be directed to do things, describes how a two-year-old not only addressed more honorifics and fewer imperatives to the older children at nursery school than to the younger, but used the same contrast to give more respect to her father than to her mother (1974). The difference may reflect a perception of relative power or familiarity with the person who usually responds to her directives; in either case, the contrast highlights how closely tuned the two-year-old is to the differences in family relationships.

The children's practical grasp of how social rules can be used to gain their own ends is seen too in their use of the rules of positive justice. They make references to sharing, taking turns, in the face of competition with siblings. These rules are also used to "get at" the sibling in a more indirect manner, as we saw in the last chapter where one boy blamed his sister for taking his mother's turn at soccer and another complained that his sister, who had run for comfort to their mother, would "hurt Mummy tea."

Moreover, children's understanding of rules of possession, evident by the middle of the second year, is employed similarly: both in direct claims about the child's rights and in arguments against the sibling's interference with the mother's possessions. That children begin to use possessive pronouns toward the end of the second year, and do so with increasing frequency in the third, is of course well established. The point to be emphasized here is the *use* that is made of the idea of possession. The motivation for many actions, again, is unclear. The children could be using the claims about rules and rights because they wish to annoy their sibling, because they want their mother's attention, because they are concerned about the mother's needs or rights, or any combination of such reasons. What is clear is the flexibility with which children use the notion of positive justice in the setting of family relationships: it is applied differently, according to the particular relationship, to the children's mood, to the sequence of previous events, and so on.

As soon as we have evidence that the children have a practical understanding of a rule, we find that they apply it differently in different relationships. To take the example of causing pain, it is clear that by 18–20 months the children understood that acts causing hurt to others were prohibited. We saw this "rule" applied in the sibling relationship in a number of ways. The operating principle appears to be: If my sibling hurts me, I can appeal for help and, because my sibling hurt me, I am likely to get it. But if I hurt my sibling, I am unlikely to get help. Children in their second year often appealed to the mother by pointing out the hurt that had been done to them.

1. Family E (Study 1). Child 21 months
Child comes to mother, crying.

M (sympathetically): Oooh!
C: Baba (her word for her brother).
M: What did your brother do?
C: Hurt.
M: Hurt? Where?
B: There (shows arm).

But, as we have seen, the children rarely appealed for help if they themselves were the aggressor. Within the mother-child relationship, the operating principle appears to be: I can tease my mother by half-hurting her, which gets attention. But if I try to hurt her, I get into trouble (see examples 1 and 13 in Chapter 3). It is crucial, of course, for the child to learn to monitor the mother's reaction, to judge how far he can go in teasing before he oversteps the limit between friendly teasing and forbidden behavior. He must learn to judge her current mood, her general disposition to teasing, and how her reaction is likely to affect others. These aspects of social relations are central to functioning happily as a family member—yet they are aspects whose development we know almost nothing about. Scattered among our observations are examples in which children and their mothers fail to "play" successfully with the themes of hurt and disobedience. Jokes between mothers and children on the themes of loving and hurting do go wrong, as we shall see in Chapter 8.

The expectation that a rule is applied differently in different relationships and situations is clear whichever rule we care to examine. For instance, the Cambridge children understood early in the second year that destructive behavior is prohibited by adults. In the sibling relationship, this understanding was evident in shared amusement and excitement between siblings when one or the other (best of all, both together) acted in the forbidden way. In some sibling pairs, it was common for the two children to engage in such escapades; each fluently read the other's invitations to the joint wickedness. But the children's grasp of the rule was equally evident when one child drew the mother's attention to the displeasing actions of the other. And with rules of positive justice, the picture is the same. As soon as the child understands the principle of turns, it is applied directly in games with the sibling, but also in more indirect attempts to get at the sibling, as shown by the example of the boy in his soccer game.

Thus children, by the second and third year, are already sensitive to how rules of approved behavior are applied in different situations, and they are also sensitive to the *generality* of such rules. When it is in their own interest to do so, they point out that a rule applied to them also applies to others. And these rules used as sources of humour, attack, and self-justification are, it must be emphasized, principles of the wider culture in which children are growing up. Already in their third year, our children are active members of a culture extending far beyond the kitchens and sitting rooms in which the family dramas take place. This membership has profound implications for the development of a sense of self.

They are only beginners, of course, in the power politics of the family-within-a-culture. The claims and excuses that young children make to support their arguments are limited in range, compared to those of slightly older children or of their mothers. By far the most common reason given, even at 26 months, is "I want." Older siblings, also under pressure to achieve their own goals, have a wider range of claims. Conversations between children provide a good way to examine which claims carry the most weight. Such a technique has been used effectively by Shweder and Much (1986). In their analysis of disputes between older preschool children, they show that each child marshals a series of excuses and claims. When one child finally concedes, following a particular claim by the other, they infer that this last claim is the one in the children's "code" that carries the greatest weight. It is of course possible that the children concede for many other reasons: they are tired of the argument, are distracted by something else, and so on. With our very young children, it is often difficult to determine why the children concede when they do. Consider the following exchange:

2. Family J (Study 3). Child 30 months
Sibling and father have been discussing rights of sibling and C to pieces of Lego.

Sib to F: They're not his bits. They're my bits. I made it. It isn't his.
C: No. Is his.
Sib to C: It isn't yours. It's mine.
C: I know.
Sib to C: 'Cos I made it. (C concedes Lego.)

This incident illustrates, first, the different justifications given by the older sibling; second, the difficulties of interpretation posed by the young child's grammar (the use of "his" in referring to himself); third, the problem of making inferences about why the child finally concedes. The sibling's claim that he should have the Lego because he made the construction is ineffective when first made and is conceded to later. To treat this exchange as a detached rational assessment of claim and counterclaim by the two siblings seems inappropriate.

In summary, it would be misleading to describe children in this age range as egocentric, inasmuch as they are quite capable of understanding that other people have feelings and intentions different from their own. My observations amply support the reports of mother-observers in the study of Radke-Yarrow, Zahn-Waxler, and Chapman (1983), reports that describe the increasing sensitivity shown by children toward distressed family members. Within this family world of familiar others, children are clearly not blinkered. They monitor with interest the relations between others, comment on and intervene in the interactions of others, cooperate with others in conflict against a third, and are able to use one family member against another. They understand something of the shared nature of family rules and of the distinctions by which such rules can be employed in different situations.

Further, the observations highlight three important points concerning the changes in children's behavior that accompany the growth of social understanding and the context in which this growth is evident. These points taken together begin to give us an account of the transition from infancy to childhood that links the striking cognitive changes reflected in the development of social understanding and the emotional changes that loom so large for parents.

Family relationships

The first point is this: the child develops social knowledge *as a family member*. It is not simply that the context of family relationships is one that reveals the child's capabilities. Rather, it may be that the special nature of children's relationships with father, mother, siblings, grandparents, and close friends if they have them (see Burlingham and Freud, 1944) elicits the development of their ability to understand other people's feelings, intentions, and relationships—and their ability to grasp the nature of authority relations, principles of justice, and so on. What drives children to read and understand their mothers' moods or their siblings' intentions, to comprehend the rules that can be used to get their own way in disputes, or to deflect punishment from themselves to others? It may be the very quality of those relationships that motivates the child to understand the family world—the emotional power of attachment and rivalry, of dominance, envy, competition, and affection.

The mother's part

My second point concerns the role of mothers' discussion of rules in the development of the child's social understanding. Our conversational analyses show that the social rules of the world in which the children were growing up were continually discussed by their mothers: discourse on what was acceptable, what unacceptable, surrounded them, and these were conversations in which they were encouraged to take part.

This is a centrally important point. The moral order of their parents' world was conveyed to the children again and again in the repeated events of their daily lives. The messages, implicit in the emotional behavior of the mother, explicit in her words, were about the moral concepts of the culture—messages in a deeply effective form. Mothers make such messages explicit *long* before children are capable of verbally expressing their own understanding of the forbidden behavior. Recall Mary reaching for the iron at 16 months and John in the incident over the toothpaste in the kitchen. I would confidently contend that both Mary and John knew that such behavior was likely to produce a prohibition, but their mothers articulated the prohibition in terms well beyond the children's powers of expression.

It is a knowledge demand on the children that may well contribute to their grasp of the rules.

From these messages, children develop their own ideas of what is acceptable and what is not. Richard Shweder and his colleagues, in their illuminating discussion of the moral ideas of children in India and in the United States, put it this way:

> Children are assisted in constructing their own notions of right and wrong. The inferences they draw about the moral (its form) and what's moral (its content) are, in substantial measure, personal reconstructions created within a framework of tradition-based modes of apperception and evaluation. The moral concepts of a people, and their ideas about self, society and nature are powerful ways of seeing the world that have been worked on, and applied to experience, over many generations. Each child is the beneficiary of a conceptual inheritance, received through communication with others. (Shweder, Mahapatra, and Miller, 1987, p. 73)

This is a point vividly made by crosscultural comparisons because the patterns and subtleties are often very different from those of our own society. Consider the Samoan children studied by Elinor Ochs (1987). Even before they are two and a half, the children in Samoa display skills of appropriate switching of the speech register in which they address familiar and nonfamiliar others. They learn in their first three years from those around them a range of cultural expectancies in speech: what is required, what is preferred, what is possible but unusual, what is awkward, and what is out of bounds altogether.

Consider too the 20-month-old Solomon Islander, observed by the Gegeos, who already greets unfamiliar visitors with gestures of hospitality and courtesy, a matter of great importance in his culture (Watson-Gegeo and Gegeo, 1987). Consider the Kipsigis children studied by Sara Harkness and Charles Super (1982) in rural Kenya: by three and four years old they are silent, respectful, and obedient to everyone older than they (they were so thoroughly a part of their culture that they caused the visiting psychologists to despair of interviewing them). As a fourth example, consider the children in the black community of Trackton, North Carolina, studied by Shirley Brice-Heath (1983). Before they were two years old, the boys had learned how to deal with public challenges, mock aggression, and teasing—how to behave in the public arena of porch and street where most of life in their community goes on. Brice-Heath comments on the social skills involved in a social world where adult reactions are inconsistent and far from muted.

> Though ostensibly the center of audience focus on many occasions, Trackton children, from a very early age, must decenter themselves in their communicative processes, for they must respond in anticipation of the behavior of those who have the power to give food, affection, and gifts. Children manage their social interactions, shifting tactics in accordance with their estimation of the audience's mood. Allowed the widest possible range of interpersonal exploration, young children can take on any role in the community. They can boss, cuss, beg, cuddle, comfort, tend, and argue with those about them; they can be old men, old women, parents, or older children in the way they communicate. (1983, p. 82)

But *which* of these roles they assume in any particular instance must be carefully judged, on the basis of others' reactions. Brice-Heath notes: "Though Trackton children's final goal is ego-centered—to provoke the most pleasant kind of interaction—they must get a sense of the other person's perspective to reach this goal. Trackton children, therefore, have to become their own strategists in these interactions, testing reactions to their actions on an almost continual basis in their human interactions" (p. 375). Already in their third year all these children are cultural selves.

Self and self-interest

My third point concerns self and self-interest. What are the developmental links between children's growing self-awareness, self-interest, and their social understanding during this period? Although our Cambridge observations showed that the children were interested in other people, and able to comprehend at a practical level some feelings of others, their driving self-interest was strikingly clear. It was evident in their increased anger and distress when confronted by mother or sibling, in their assertiveness and refusal to comply with these others, in their resistance to those who prevented the achievement of their goals, in the nature of their reasoning and excuses ("I want," "It's mine," "My turn"), in the emotion and sophisticated reasoning generated over conflicts of possessions and rights.

Perhaps paradoxically, research in the United States and Britain on the development of compliance over this period confirms the point that a child's self-interest continues to have major significance. It has been repeatedly reported that parents make frequent attempts to control their children in the second and third year—whether at home or in a laboratory situation—but that these attempts are complied with less than 50 percent of the time (Londerville and Main, 1980; Lytton, 1977; Lytton and Zwirner, 1975; McGlaughlin, 1983; Minton, Kagan, and Levine, 1971; Schaffer and Crook, 1979). But though some aspects of compliance increase between 18 and 30 months, argumentative noncompliance *increases* (Vaughn, Kopp, and Krakow, 1984). Moreover, the likelihood of compliance seems to depend strongly on whether the mother's directive is solicited by and benefits the child (Matas, Arend, and Sroufe, 1978), on whether the child is already interested in the object of the mother's directive (Schaffer and Crook, 1979), and on whether the mother has previously complied with the child. Thus Mary Parpal and Eleanor Maccoby (1985) found that children who had previously participated in a "child-directed" play session with their mothers complied more with their mothers in a later task than children who had participated in a "natural" mother-child play session. Our Cambridge observations, however, do more than confirm the centrality of self-interest to children of this age (western children, at least) and their acute and increasing awareness of self. They open up a new perspective on the developmental significance of this new sense of self and of the power of self-interest.

The willfullness and difficult behavior of two-year-olds, of course, has often been linked to the child's developing sense of self. It has been argued that because children have an increasingly clear and articulated sense of themselves and a new pleasure in autonomy and independence, they feel a new sense of frustration at interference or attempts to direct them. Changes in children's self-awareness over this age period have been documented in terms of mirror recognition (Berenthal and Fischer, 1978; Lewis and Brooks-Gunn, 1979), in response to failure to achieve desired effects or to imitate adult modeling (Kagan, 1981), in the use of self-descriptive terms linguistically, and in other ways (see, for instance, the blanket test in Heckhausen, 1983). These different tests give a concordant picture of increasing self-awareness during the second year, especially between 18 and 24 months. In commonsense terms it seems reasonable to link the two-year-old's fury when he is frustrated to this new sense of himself and his own powers.

A rather different view of the increase in tantrums and difficult behavior links this increase in anger and distress to a "developmental dilemma" over this period (Heckhausen, 1983). According to this theory, there is a discrepancy between the rapid development of children's ability to develop goals and the much slower growth of their ability to communicate their plans or to face delay. The two developmental accounts are not incompatible: the development of the ability to plan goals and a growing awareness of self might well combine to give children a heightened sense of self-interest, a preoccupation with their own concerns. But in both accounts there is a striking gap. There is very little consideration of the relation of these developments to emotional experiences. Accounts of changes in children's self-awareness, for instance, are essentially maturational. Changes in children's responses to self-in-mirror or to adult interferences are usually described in stage terms, for a mythical child who grows up alone. The implications are that the cognitive abilities of the child simply emerge with age. Questions about how emotional experiences or social relationships might contribute to developmental changes are seldom asked, and indeed are irrelevant to such accounts. Although changes in self-awareness are seen as leading to emotional development (Lewis and Brooks-Gunn, 1979), influences from emotional experiences are rarely commented upon (but see Izard, 1978, on the contribution of shame and embarrassment to self-awareness). And questions about the effect of changes in self-awareness on the child's social understanding have been examined only in crude terms. Social knowledge in terms of age and gender categorization, yes, but in terms of understanding a culture's moral precepts—hardly. In fact such questions are inappropriate, as long as children are viewed as incapable of perceiving the feelings and intentions of others.

In contrast, I am arguing here for two considerations in relation to the development of a sense of self: the first concerns links between self-awareness and awareness of others: the second, connections between self-awareness and emotional experiences.

Awareness of others

Some psychoanalytic accounts do emphasize that an increase in self-awareness must involve a parallel increase in awareness of others. According to René Spitz, "The beginning awareness of the self is predicated on the awareness of the 'other' " (1957, p. 130). Indeed Spitz stresses the significance of children's opposition to their mothers, during the second year, in their awareness of both self and other:

> The acquisition of the "No" is the indicator of a new level of autonomy, of the awareness of the "other" and of the awareness of the self; it is the beginning of the restructuration of mentation on the higher level of complexity; it initiates an extensive ego development, in the framework of which the dominance of the reality principle over the pleasure principle becomes increasingly established. (p. 129)

These changes in awareness of the other are not specified, however, and the idea has not been taken up in any detail by developmental psychologists. Surely it should be. Let us consider for a moment the development of a sense of self as it is viewed within a different intellectual tradition, that of the sociologist George Herbert Mead (1934). Within Mead's theoretical framework, the exploration of the processes involved in the developing sense of self is a central issue. The growth of self-awareness is seen as culturally linked to the child's understanding of others. To have a sense of self is to have the ability to think about oneself from the standpoint of another. Thus some grasp of how others respond to and perceive one is the foundation for the developing sense of self. In contrast to the developmental psychologist's approach, within the Meadian framework the self is seen as the product of the individual's social exchange with others. Initially it is the child's view of how a particular other sees him or her that is significant in the developing sense of self, but with time it is the child's view of the "generalized other" of the wider cultural group that becomes important.

Now a clear division is often made between, on the one hand, self-awareness in terms of "categorical self"—say awareness of gender and age—which is seen as the product of cognitive changes in the second and third years, and, on the other hand, self-evaluation in terms of goodness, competence, and worth, qualities linked to social comparisons and to the child's reflection on self in terms of what is valued by others. This self-evaluation is considered a later development, socially influenced, and is treated as a separate component of the developing self (see, for instance, Kagan, 1984, p. 138).

But such a dichotomy may be misleading. I suggest that we should consider bringing together the developmental psychologists' experimental evidence for growing self-awareness and a Meadian view of self-as-product-of-society. This is to argue that, during the second and third year, children are sensitive to the responses of others (approval, support, disapproval) to themselves and to others (they are for example beginning to comment on these responses with questions and jokes). It is to argue that sensitivity to others is central to developing self-awareness: the self that develops is—even in the second and third year—a product of culture as well as of cognitive change. What is striking about the observations I have documented here is their theoretical significance for the Meadian view. The observations of the Cambridge children, and those of Samoa, Kenya, North Carolina, and the Solomon Islands, show that during the second and third years the children were indeed sensitive to central tenets of their particular culture—a world beyond the family but affecting them through their family relationships. The polite and hospitable Solomon Islander, the Samoan two-year-old deftly switching speech registers, the obedient Kipsigis children, the boldly teasing Trackton boys, the Cambridge child demanding her vacuum cleaner because she's a lady—all are, as selves, members of specific cultures. For each, a sense of self-efficacy comes from managing a particular cultural world; all gain pleasure from their own mastery of the difficulties—social and psychological—that face them, their own powers within that world.

Emotional experiences

Such an account implies that social interaction is central to the development of children's sense of self and of their particular world. What about the role of emotional experiences in such developments? I suggest that questions about how emotional experiences contribute both to the development of self-awareness and to an understanding of others are indeed worth asking. First, consider the emotion expressed by children when their goals are frustrated. Such displays increased in frequency between 14 and 21 months, just at the period when the child's sense of self changes so markedly. The parallels in development are notable. Links between emotion and cognitive change are usually viewed in terms of the cognitive changes that underlie emotional development—the close connection between the two is acknowledged and unquestioned. But in discussions of the nature of that connection, the emphasis has been overwhelmingly upon the role of cognition in emotional development. It is clear that the development of joy, fear, anger, shame, embarrassment, and surprise all depend upon cognitive changes in the child (Sroufe, 1979). And evidence for the development of pride, shame, and guilt during the third year is clearly relevant to the argument that the cognitive basis for children's sense of self and other expands rapidly over this period.

In contrast, the possibility that emotional experiences themselves contribute to cognitive change has been seldom considered, in spite of the demonstration that the emotional context of an experience profoundly affects the way in which it is remembered and has a bearing on current functioning (Bower, 1980; Maccoby and Martin, 1983). Especially relevant here is a study of first- and third-graders' conception of moral issues, which demonstrated that the emotion the children experienced in connection with particular events was strongly related to their memory of such events and to their coding and differentiation of the events (Arsenio and Ford, 1985). Our observations of children in conflict with their siblings and mothers show that it is in those contexts where the children so often expressed anger or distress that they later were likely to reason rather than simply protest. So the association raises the possibility that it is in part *because* of the emotion experienced in these encounters that the children were attentive to the other's behavior, watched with heightened vigilance, remembered, reflected on, and learned from the memories of those exchanges. What has to be explained is the striking growth in understanding demonstrated in just those family exchanges in which the children had earlier expressed and presumably experienced intense emotions. The discrepancy between the capabilities that young children display when making judgments about hypothetical or storybook characters, in conventional empathy or judgmental tasks, and their capabilities in real-life family dramas could well be linked to the emotional significance of those family encounters.

Now consider the relation between a child's social knowledge and the developments in sense of self. The contexts in which the Cambridge children demonstrated their understanding of social rules, of authority relations, of the feelings of others, justice, and their most advanced reasoning were not propositional disputes, but settings in which their own self-interest was threatened. These were settings of frustration when one might well have expected the children simply to howl or hit, to regress to early patterns of demand. Instead, by three years we find the children marshaling some very sophisticated reasoning. It is possible that the child's self-interest at least partly motivates her attempts to understand the social world. My proposal, then, is that situations of conflict and threatened self-interest are encounters in which the child's growing understanding of the social world is not only revealed but fostered. A similar point is made by Dennie Wolf in discussing the development of the child's understanding of agency during the second year:

> In the earliest period, children combine their existing understanding of agency and the physical separateness of others into an ability to use others, although not exclusively, as auxiliaries or "tools" for the accomplishment of personal plans. In part, possibly, because others do not always wholly or successfully submit to being used as extensions of the self, children become aware of the relations between self and other and thus alive to some similarities between human agents. (1982, p. 304)

Freud, writing on the child's self-love and the later development of the ability to love others, said that "his egoism has taught him to love" (1966, p. 204). What I propose here is that a child's egoism, in the context of family relationships, motivates him *to understand others.* I would emphasize again that to suggest that these motivational and emotional issues are important in the development of social understanding is *not* to argue against the significance of cognitive mechanisms. Of course cognitive change is involved in cognitive achievements. The argument is rather that such cognitive change may not be independent of motivational and emotional processes; a simple dichotomy between cognitive and emotional or motivational processes is coming under increasing criticism from psychologists of very different backgrounds.

In examining the connection between egoism and social understanding, we must look beyond situations of conflict, in which a child's self-interest is inevitably threatened. What about the evidence for the development of empathetic and prosocial behavior, children's compliance and cooperative actions? These are actions that surely are not self-interested, and they depend on understanding the feelings and needs of others. In the next chapters I shall examine these features of the children's behavior with three issues in mind: What do they show us about the nature of children's social understanding? How is this social understanding linked to the children's relationships with their mothers and siblings? And do these aspects of children's behavior shed light on the relation of self-interest to the development of social understanding?

5

Benevolent Babies?

It seems a happiness in the present theory, that it enters not
into that vulgar dispute concerning the *degrees* of benevolence
or self-love, which prevail in human nature . . . It is sufficient
for our present purpose, if it be allowed, what surely, without
the greatest absurdity cannot be disputed, that there is some
benevolence, however small, infused in our bosom; some spark
of friendship for human kind; some particle of the dove
kneaded into our frame, along with the elements of the wolf
and serpent.

—David Hume, *Enquiries concerning the Human Understanding and concerning the Principles of Morals,* 1777

The argument proposed in the last chapter was that
children between one and three years of age show considerable
practical understanding of the feelings and intentions of other
family members, but that their own self-interest is itself an important driving force that can contribute to their capacity to
understand the social world. This argument, however, was based
on observation of a relatively narrow area of children's behavior.
If children are indeed able to recognize feelings and understand
social rules in the second and third year, this should profoundly
affect other aspects of their behavior and their relationships—for
instance, their response to distress in others, their concern for
others' feelings, their ability to cooperate, help, and share. Children who understand how to upset others, and how to enlist the
aid of adults in their disputes, presumably should also be able to
act empathetically toward those others. Do we have evidence for
such empathetic or cooperative behavior in very young children?
And if children do indeed show concern for others and are eager
to share, how is this concern compatible with the "self-love" so
evident in their conflict behavior? Do we have evidence for some

particle of the dove, as Hume suggested, along with the elements of the wolf and serpent that are all too clearly present?

The question of how, when, and why children begin to show empathetic concern for others and to cooperate is an interesting and important one for parents and for psychologists. It brings us, head on, to the vexed issue of whether small children are indeed selfish original sinners or whether they are, as some psychologists now maintain, quite the opposite—"benevolent babies" (Bridgeman, 1983), naturally eager to cooperate, concerned about the feelings of others from an early age. At issue are two questions: the point at which children begin to *act* in a way that benefits others; and the motivation of such behavior. People can, of course, behave in a way that is "prosocial" for a wide variety of reasons: not only because they are concerned about the feelings or needs of another, but in order to ingratiate themselves with others, to dominate or assert themselves, to engage someone's attention, to become part of a group, to obey a rule or convention, and so on. Those who wish to characterize children either as benevolent or as amoral creatures in need of civilizing need first to establish why children do what they do.

Observers of children have frequently commented on early signs of sensitivity to others' needs and emotions. Lewin (1942), Guillaume (1926), Isaacs (1924), Piaget (1932), Stern (1924), and Sullivan (1940) all concluded that children showed some affective sensitivity or sympathy in the first two years. Sully (1896) writes at length on children's early responsiveness to distress in others, especially to pain in animals. These writers stress both the empathic sensing of the mood of another and the sympathetic identification with another's distress. As William Stern put it:

> Even the two year old child has the power of feeling another's sorrow, not only in the sense that, infected by the other's feelings, he grows sad and anxious with him and cries in response to the other's tears (i.e. suggested emotion), but in the higher sense of putting himself in the other's place, identifying with his sorrow, pain or fear, and trying to comfort, help or even avenge him. (1924, p. 521)

But those who kept detailed diaries also comment on the capriciousness with which very young children change from showing kindness to disregard for others' feelings, and on the wide individual differences between children in their sensitivity to feelings. Sully comments wryly on the child (C.) in *Studies of Childhood*:

It is sad going through the pages of the diary [of the child's father] to note that there is scarcely any observation during this second year on the development of kindly feelings. One would have supposed that with all the affection and care lavished on him C. might have manifested a little tenderness in response. The only incident put down under the head of social feeling in this year is the following (aet. twenty months): "When he eats porridge in the morning at family breakfast he takes a look round and says: 'Mamma, Tit, papa, Ningi', appearing to be pleased at finding himself sharing a common enjoyment." This (continues the narrator) is a step onward from the antisocial attitude which he took up not long since when some of his mother's egg was given to his sister and he shouted prohibitively: "No! No!" (1896, p. 433)

This is hardly impressive evidence for the development of empathetic sensitivity—Sully's final comment on the issue is that "the worthy parent appears to be making the most of very small mercies here." But against such observations are ranged consistent accounts of sympathetic behavior occurring over the same age period, often in the same children who were also on occasion callous or unkind. Anna Freud's and Dorothy Burlingham's observations of the young children brought up together in the Hampstead Nursery, in the Second World War, clearly document the consoling, tender, and helpful behavior these very young children showed to one another, as well as the outbreaks of aggression between them. The following observations are typical:

Edith (21 months) had been hurt by Paul (23 months) and cried bitterly. When Sam (20 months) saw Edith unhappy, he came to comfort her; Larry (19 months) watched the scene and went to help Sam to comfort Edith . . .

Sam (20 months) was playing peacefully . . . when suddenly Larry (19 months) took his ball away. Sam looked at his empty hands helplessly and began to cry. Edith (21 months) had watched this scene; she rushed over to Larry, bit him, took the ball away from him, brought the ball back to Sam, and stroked his hair until he was comforted . . .

The nurse who had entered the rest room during the children's afternoon nap found Paul (2 years) and Sophie (19 months) standing at one end of their cots kissing each other. She was amused and laughed. Paul turned around and smiled at her for a moment, then again held Sophie's head between both his hands and kissed her over and over again. Sophie smiled and was obviously pleased . . .

Sophie (20 months) stood in a corner of the nursery and looked at Larry (19 months). Larry noticed her and went to her saying "Ay! ay!" Sophie put her arms around Larry. They stayed like that for quite a while. (1944, pp. 573, 584)

In the first study of siblings that we conducted (Dunn and Kendrick, 1982), we were struck by some incidents in which very young second-born children attempted to comfort their older siblings:

Several incidents suggested that during the second year children begin to recognize that the distress of others can be relieved by the provision of comfort, but that what constitutes comfort for the other is not necessarily identical to that which would constitute comfort for the child himself. There appears to be an awareness as early as 14 to 15 months that some of the acts within the child's power can provide some comfort for others, but the child may well overgeneralize the types of occasion or person for whom the action can be expected to provide comfort. Take for instance the following incident, which occurred when a 15-month-old was in the garden with his brother. The 15-month-old, Len, was a stocky boy with a fine round tummy, and he played at this time a particular game with his parents which always made him laugh. His game was to come towards them, walking in an odd way, pulling up his T-shirt and showing his big stomach. One day his elder brother fell off the climbing frame in the garden and cried vigorously. Len watched solemnly. Then he approached his brother, pulling up his T-shirt and showing his tummy, vocalizing, and looking at his brother. (p. 115)

Such observations suggest that children early in the second year are sensitive to others' needs and that they do sometimes attempt to comfort those in distress. What do the systematic observations of present-day psychologists reveal on the beginnings of empathy?

As with the other features of children's social understanding, we find a gap in systematic research between the scattering of studies on infants' responses to others' emotions and the wealth of research on cooperative and prosocial behavior among preschool and older children. There is a substantial literature on the development of prosocial behavior in children from three years on, comprehensively summarized in a recent book by Nancy Eisenberg (1986). But for the period between the first year of life and the group life of children in preschool, there is (at the time of writing) in addition to the Cambridge studies only one study of response to emotion that includes children between one year and two, in their families, and only three semi-naturalistic studies of sharing and cooperation (Bridgeman, 1983; Rheingold, Hay, and West, 1976; Stanjek, 1978). Yet, as the early writers and the findings of these studies show, it is during the second year that children first begin to act with sympathy toward others.

Response to distress

If we are to make inferences about what children understand of another's distress then, as Eisenberg has pointed out, it is important to distinguish three different forms of reaction, all of which have been termed empathy. The first is an emotional reaction in which the individual feels the same emotion as the other person but is not clearly directed to help, a response sometimes termed "emotional contagion." The second is a response in which the individual responds to the emotion of another in a manner that is congruent with and shows a concern for the welfare of that other, or "sympathetic responding." And third there is a form of reaction that has been labeled "personal distress," in which the individual shows a concern that is focused upon him- or herself rather than upon the distressed other.

The distress of a sibling

During the first weeks of life, babies show a sensitivity to the crying and distress of other babies: they are likely to cry in response (Sagi and Hoffman, 1976; Simner, 1971). Later in the first year, the picture is more complicated. One study of 6-month-olds repoɪ̣ɪs little response to the distress of peers (Hay, Nash, and Pedersen, 1981). But from 10 months on, children quite often respond to the crying of other children by crying themselves (Bridges, 1932; Zahn-Waxler and Radke-Yarrow, 1982). These infant reactions are usually thought of as emotional contagion and do not imply any concern for the welfare of others. Yet, over the early months of the second year, this response changes, as Radke-Yarrow's and Zahn-Waxler's important work reveals.

In that study, three groups of children, aged 10, 15, and 20 months, were followed for nine months each. Mothers were trained to record in detail the response of the children to naturally occurring incidents of other people's distress. At 10 and 12 months, in about half the incidents the children showed some agitation: frowning, looking sad, checking with the mother. "Over the next six to eight months the behavior changed. General agitation began to wane, concerned attention remained prominent, and positive initiations to others in distress began to appear . . . Such contacts became increasingly differentiated and frequent by 18 to 24 months of age" (Radke-Yarrow, Zahn-Waxler, and Chapman, 1983, p. 481).

As two-year-olds, the study continues, many children made considerable effort to comfort and alleviate the distress of another. They fetched people to help, brought objects to the distressed person, made suggestions about what to do, and attempted to cheer up the other. If one method failed, they tried different strategies. Such behavior clearly reflects a recognition of the other person's distress and a sympathetic attempt to alleviate it. Sometimes the children did show less sympathetic responses, avoiding the distressed person or even attacking him. But these personal-distress reactions were less common than the sympathetic responses. It should be noted that, although these results were from mothers' reports, videotaped records of the response of children to simulated distress by the mothers confirmed the general pattern of findings.

In the observations we made in Cambridge, distress was predominantly shown by the children and their siblings rather than by adults. The picture of response to sibling distress is one that complements but in important respects differs from that drawn by Radke-Yarrow and Zahn-Waxler.

First, it was clear that as early as 14 months children were on occasion upset by the distress of their sibling. Generalized distress that apparently fitted the contagious-empathy description was quite often the response of the youngest children studied—those of 14 and 16 months. But several other reactions were also observed. Among the reactions of 14- and 16-month-olds in Study 1 were the following: child begins to cry himself (Families N, B); child sobers and hides face (Family C); child looks at mother (Family D); child points to sibling, vocalizes, pulls mother toward sibling (Family B); child inspects own body part, similar to hurt part of sibling (Families C, B, D, H); child pats sibling (Families C, D). In several instances the children simply ignored or watched the siblings crying without taking any action.

In the following months, the children sometimes made clear attempts to comfort. Very often their mothers became involved in the incidents, drew the children's attention to the sibling's distress, and suggested that the children should give comfort. Note in the next example that the mother emphasizes the accidental nature of the hurt.

1. Family D (Study 1). Child 21 months
C is playing a game of jumping off chair arm to cushion
on floor. She jumps and with her shoe accidentally hits
sibling, who cries. M comforts sibling. C comes to sibling
with concerned expression, strokes her head.

M to sib: Oh, did you get kicked? (To C) You'll have to be

more careful with those great shoes, Nan. (To sib) Does it
still hurt?
Sib (crying): Yes.
M to C: Say sorry to Clare?
C to sib: Sorry (kisses and strokes her).
M to sib: It was a mistake. She didn't mean to, darling. It was
an accident.

2. Family R (Study 2). Child 18 months
Sibling is crying bitterly, lying on M's knee, face down.
M attempts to comfort. C watches soberly.

M to C: What's wrong with Kelly?
(C, with concerned expression, bends down, turns his head to
look face to face at sib, strokes her hair.)

The children did not always act in such a caring way. They
often ignored the distress, and by 24 months there were several
instances (when they themselves had been responsible for causing the distress) in which they laughed or even acted in such a
way as to increase the distress of the other. For the forty children observed at 18, 24, and 36 months in Study 2, we distin-
guished five main categories of response: ignoring, watching,
attempts to comfort (which included attempts to get adult aid
for the distressed sibling), laughing, and exacerbating the distress. The results are shown in Figs. 5.1 and 5.2.

There was a substantial difference in how the children and
their siblings responded to distress, depending upon whether
they themselves had caused the distress. The same child in some
cases responded by showing concern if she or he had not been
involved in causing the distress, but by laughing or exacerbating
the upset if responsible for the initial distress. It is clear that by
18 months most children recognized the distressed feelings of
their sibling and that they were capable either of making an
attempt to alleviate the distress or of exacerbating it. Children
of this age *can* comfort but, as far as their sibling is concerned,

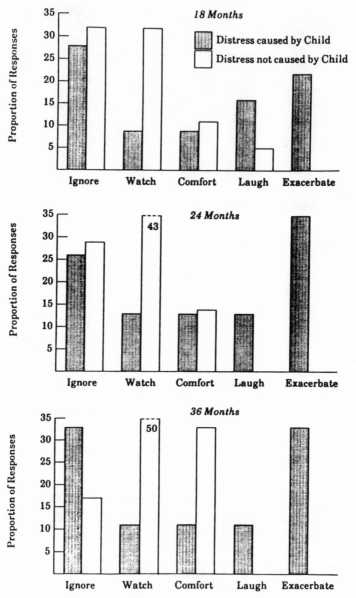

Fig. 5.1 Proportion of different child responses to sibling
distress (Study 2)

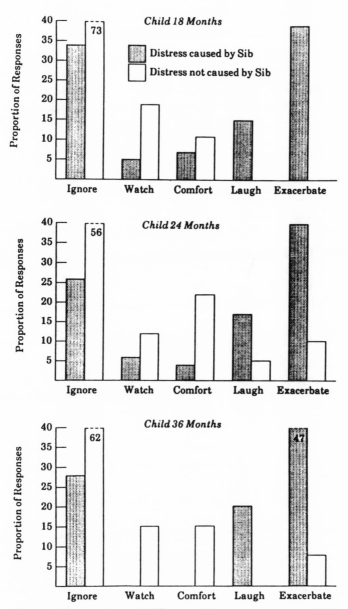

Fig. 5.2 Proportion of different sibling responses to child distress (Study 2)

they are rarely motivated to do so. Indeed they quite often attempt to increase rather than alleviate the distress.

What is striking is that, as Fig. 5.1 shows, there are no increases with age in the probability that children will comfort their distressed siblings. The second-born 18-month-olds were as likely as their older siblings (whose average age was 45 months) to attempt to comfort (Fig. 5.2). At 36 months there were too few incidents of sibling distress to justify differentiation of the children's responses. Note, however, that at this stage the siblings, now aged on average 5 and a half years, were not significantly more likely to comfort the other child than their siblings had been as 18-month-olds.

If they did make attempts to comfort, the children in their third year usually made more elaborate attempts than they had when they were younger. In the next example, the older brother Len is crying because his mother scolded him and refused to comfort him after he had bitten his younger brother. Jay, although the injured party, is quite concerned about his brother's distress and tries a number of different ways to stop his crying— first trying to get their mother to comfort him, then patting him, then helping him, speaking to him with an affectionate diminutive, attempting to distract him, and finally imitating his mother's threat to smack him if he doesn't stop crying.

3. Family J (Study 3). Child 30 months
Sibling is crying, C attempts to comfort.

C to sib: Len. Don't——stop crying, mate. Stop it crying.
C to M: Len crying, Mummy! Len crying. Look. Me show you. Len crying.
C to sib: Look, Len. No go on crying (pats sib) . . . (Sib still sobs.) Ah Len (helps sib with Lego bag). I put it back for Lennie, hey? . . . (Shows sib a car) There's this man in here. What's this, Len? What's this, Len? (Sib sobs.)
M to sib: Do you want me to smack you?
Sib to M: No.
M: Then just stop it, please.

Sib to M: I'm trying to (sobs) . . .
C to sib (still crying): Stop crying, Len. Smack your bottom.

The motivation of the children who did attempt to comfort their siblings is in many instances difficult to interpret. Take, for instance, an incident from the first sibling study we conducted (Dunn and Kendrick, 1982). Firstborn children were followed over the period when a second child was born; in the months that followed the sibling birth, many of the children showed considerable concern when their baby siblings cried—though others reacted with glee, as Fig. 5.3 shows.

In one observation, the 8-month-old baby was crying and his 30-month-old sibling offered him a cracker. The action might well be interpreted as showing some concern for the baby's distress and be described as comforting. But the mother commented that she thought the child was trying to keep a parent from paying attention to the baby and was not concerned about the baby's well-being. As I have said, how seriously an observer takes such an interpretation would depend largely on the par-

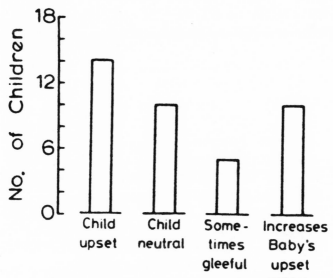

Fig. 5.3 Reaction of firstborn child when secondborn baby is upset (Study 4)

ticular theory held by the observer. Such theories range from a willingness to attribute only the simplest of motives to an enthusiasm among some psychoanalysts for attributing motives of great complexity. It is unlikely that a reaction of distress when a baby sibling cries reflects simple affectionate concern: the children who most frequently showed distress when the baby cried were *not* those who were in other ways most affectionate. Rather, they were those children who were most easily worried and agitated. The point that young children respond in complex and ambivalent ways to the distress of other children, amply demonstrated in our first sibling study, was also emphasized by Margaret Mahler and her colleagues (1975). In a clinical study of five babies followed from 5 months to three years, they showed that the same 18-month-old who, on one occasion gave his bottle to a crying baby, on another occasion responded to the baby's distress with an aggressive attack.

Distressed parents

Incidents in which the mothers and fathers expressed distress or pain occurred infrequently in our observations. But the children's response to these few incidents support the findings reported by the mothers in the study by Zahn-Waxler and Radke-Yarrow (1982). In contrast to their apparent unconcern about sibling distress, the children never failed to note a parent in pain. The slightest incident was commented upon and often reported to the other parent.

4. Family J (Study 3). Child 28 months
Father is working with screwdriver and hurts his wrist.

F: Oooh!
C: It hurt you, Dad?
F: No, I just twisted me wrist.
C to O: He——like that. Boink! Daddy——boink. (To M)
  Dad hurt his finger.
M: Daddy hurt his finger?
C: Yes.

Attempts to comfort parents by children who were midway through their second year were simple: presenting their own comfort objects to their mothers, stroking, patting. In the third year, attempts were more elaborate and included two-and-a-half-year-olds trying to fetch the other parent, bringing first-aid boxes, and showing much physical affection. While the children were, as we have seen, great teasers of their mothers, they were concerned when the teasing seemed to cause distress as opposed to mild irritation or crossness, and they were not always adept at judging real from pretend crying by their mothers. In the next example the 24-month-old John hastily concedes when his mother pretends to cry.

4. *Family N (Study 2). Child 24 months*
Child prohibits M from building with his bricks.

C: No no no!
M: No? Can't I build a little building? Here, look. A little station.
C: No. No.
M: Oh all right then (pretends to cry). I want to play! At building!
C: No you can't . . . (Looks concerned at M) You can!
M: That's kind of you, John.
C: Yes you can! Yes you can!

By three years old, John was not so misled by his mother's pretend crying. In the next example, taken from an observation one year after the building incident just noted, John's mother is playing with his older sister. She had made a pretend lollipop out of a construction kit and, when she pretends to eat it, John intervenes with a protest. In the ensuing argument he wavers only at the threat of no birthday cake.

5. *Family N (Study 2). Child 36 months*
C refers to construction-kit lollipop M is pretending to eat.

C to M: No they're not to do that with. They're not to do that with.

M: Why?

C: 'Cos I don't want you doing that with them.

M: Why?

C: Because I don't want you doing that with them. (He breaks the lollipop.)

M: (pretends to cry): It was a nice thing.

C: It wasn't a nice thing.

M: It *was* a nice thing.

Sib: It *was* a nice thing.

C: It isn't. I don't think it is. I don't think it is.

M: (pretending to be upset still): I think you're rotten.

C: Gone! Gone! Gone! Gone! Gone! Gone! Gone! You can't have it . . .

M: How about I won't make you a nice birthday cake for your birthday party?

C: Yes. Make one of those. You *can* make one of those. You *can* make one of those (gives her back the construction-kit items).

Sib: Make one for her.

C: I'll get all the yellow ones.

Here comforting was provided not at the cost of the child's own interests but in the service of those threatened interests. These results on the response to sibling and parental distress show that it would be a mistake to talk of "the" empathetic behavior of a child and to look for developmental changes in this behavior without reference to particular relationships. The capability of these children to recognize and respond to the distress of others parallels that described by the mothers in Radke-Yarrow and Zahn-Waxler's study—but the motivation to act on that capability clearly differs in different relationships and in different incidents within the same relationship.

It is important to note, too, that children of around 24 months can respond in a practical and appropriate way not only to those who are in evident distress or pain, but to those who are in a difficult or unhappy situation or who want something. Consider the following examples, from Larry Blum's discussion of moral behavior (1987):

> Sarah, 2 years 3 months, is riding in the car with her cousin Ali, who is 4. Ali is upset because she does not have her teddy bear, and there is a fairly extended discussion about how the bear is probably in the trunk and can be retrieved when they arrive at the house. About ten minutes pass and as the car approaches the house Sarah says to Ali, "Now you can get your bear" . . .
>
> Sarah, 3, gives Clara, 3, her own Donald Duck hat (to keep "forever"), saying that she has done so because Clara has (recently, but not at the moment) lost her (Boston) Celtics cap.

As Blum comments, Sarah "responds not to an immediate state of distress of the other child but draws on her memory and knowledge of the other child's condition . . . Sarah's responsiveness is not to a specific state of *distress* but rather simply to what she believes Clara wants or would like" (p. 310).

Sharing and helping

No parent and no observer can fail to be aware of how often very young children show, offer, and give objects to others. Often such gestures appear to be social overtures, friendly actions or attempts to engage another in interaction. As soon as children can walk, they will stagger over to someone, especially if that person is unfamiliar, and offer an object. Sometimes the proffered object is in fact withdrawn if the person attempts to take it, and the gesture remains ambiguous. Precisely how such actions should be interpreted is unclear, though their friendly sociable quality is unquestionable. Indeed these actions have been interpreted very differently by various psychologists. On the one hand, they have been seen as attention-seeking, approval-seeking acts, indices of dependency; or they have been classed as signs of children's eagerness to "freely *offer* their own attention, affection, sympathy, help, and possessions to others" (Rheingold and Hay, 1978, p. 119).

Harriet Rheingold and her colleagues hold this view of the prosocial behavior of babies on the basis of a series of studies of children's giving and sharing behavior, carried out in a suite of homelike rooms set up within a laboratory. Almost all of the 15- and 18-month-old children were observed to show objects, give objects, or attempt to engage another person in play with objects, and these behaviors, which increased in frequency with age, were considered by the researchers to be acts of sharing. In one study the mothers of two-year-olds were engaged in tasks in these rooms—sweeping, folding laundry, setting a table. All of the children attempted to help their mothers in these tasks, unasked, and many of their helping acts were innovative rather than imitative. The findings make clear how interested the children were in their mothers' tasks; their innovative actions show that they understood something of what their mothers were trying to accomplish and were both able and willing to contribute to those goals.

These studies, and other observations such as those of children in a waiting room by Stanjek (1978), demonstrate just how sociable children are at this age. The gift giving of the youngest children in Stanjek's study—involving objects such as pieces of wood and stones—is most plausibly seen as an attempt to start social interaction. While mothers of children of this age often lament their children's unwillingness to "play on their own," developmental psychologists welcome such signs of the natural sociability and friendliness of children. But whether such acts of giving should be termed *sharing* seems questionable. What about sharing that involves giving up something that is more evidently a valued good? How does sharing behavior within the family develop?

Here again there is a striking gap in our information. Of the forty studies of sharing that are tabulated in the review of prosocial behavior by Radke-Yarrow, Zahn-Waxler, and Chapman (1983), only two include children under three years old— and neither employs observation of children at home. Studies of preschool children in a nursery often include sharing behavior, though this is frequently conflated with measures of other prosocial behavior. In Lois B. Murphy's classic study (1937) of nursery-school children, in which each child was observed for three hours, sympathetic acts that included sharing, helping, and comforting were shown on average at a rate of just under one per hour. Other studies report slightly more frequent prosocial actions among preschoolers (for instance, Eisenberg-Berg and Hand, 1979; Yarrow and Waxler, 1976; Strayer, Wareing, and Rushton, 1979). The rates of prosocial behavior differ widely, however, according to the nature of behavior included within the category.

In Cambridge Study 2 we defined sharing acts as those in which the child gives away or allows temporary use of a material object previously in the child's possession, and we differentiated between solicited and unsolicited sharing. (Solicited sharing included those incidents in which the child was requested or instructed to share by the mother.) Helping acts were those in which a child attempted to alleviate another's nonemotional needs, by giving information, helping with a task, offering an object, and so on. Just over half of the children were observed to share or help in this way at 18, 24, and 36 months, yet there were no striking increases in the frequency of such actions between 18 and 36 months. But the older siblings were significantly more likely to help their younger siblings than vice versa at each age point, although rates of unsolicited sharing by child and by sibling were similar. Results from nursery-school children are inconsistent on this point, but at least one study has shown that sharing increases with age between four and five years old (Eisenberg-Berg and Hand, 1979).

The frequency of such acts was not high. On average, both children and siblings shared in about 2 percent of their interactions at each of the three time points, and the older siblings helped the younger in about 5 percent of interactions. By the time they were 36 months old, the secondborn children attempted to help their siblings or give them something they needed in about 2 percent of their exchanges. It is clear that these children do understand when their sibling wants what they have—recall their behavior in conflict over possessions.

But the motivation to share frequently is not great. Some children, indeed, even object when their sibling is given things that they themselves *don't* want (examples 7 and 8 in Chapter 3 and Sully's comments on the child C.).

Two further points stand out from Study 2. First, there were great individual differences between children in their willingness to share. Some are described by their mothers as sharing happily and willingly, without any coercion. Others apparently hate to share even their oldest possessions. Our interviews showed that mothers differ markedly in their attitude to sharing and possessions. Some claimed that the children had very few possessions of their own and openly discouraged discussion of possession. Others were careful to delineate what belonged to whom and hoped to teach the children respect for other people's property.

The second point is that there are important differences in how willing children are to share, depending on the particular object at issue. Almost all the children shared food and candy readily, and they were under great pressure from their parents to do so. The message that "if *you* have a cookie, your sister must also have one" was repeatedly stressed from the earliest observations. The result was that even the youngest children often immediately gave a share of candy, cake, or biscuit to their sibling; if they alone were offered such goodies, they frequently asked where the sibling's share was, even in families where the siblings were very hostile to one another—as in the next example. Denny is the older brother, with whom the child is constantly fighting.

6. *Family C (Study 2). Child 24 months*
C demands drink.

C: Drink.
M: You're only having a little more. Then that's all. All right?
C: Denny drink.
M: Well, you ask Denny if he wants one. Do you want a drink?
C: Denny drink.

M: Don't you worry about him. He won't get left out.
C: More drink.
M: Mummy'll get it.

In contrast to this readiness to share food and drink, several were less happy to share toys or games and, if their mothers insisted, obeyed very unwillingly. The disputes between siblings, described in Chapter 3, were most frequently focused upon the issue of sharing possessions.

Why do children share and help each other?

The motivation behind very young children's acts of sharing and helping is difficult to explore. Even when we can ask children why they acted in a particular way, some ambiguities remain. Nancy Eisenberg has carried out an imaginative series of studies of the prosocial behavior and moral reasoning of four- and five-year-olds, research that begins to illuminate the motivation of children slightly older than those we observed in Cambridge. Eisenberg and her colleagues explored the relations between the spontaneous sharing, comforting, and helping behavior of nursery-school children, their own explanations of why they behaved in these ways (elicited by the observer after a prosocial incident), and their moral reasoning about hypothetical dilemmas presented to them in stories.

In explaining their own behavior, the children referred most frequently to the needs of others and gave pragmatic (non-moral) reasons for the actions. Explanations in terms of friendship, mutual benefit, and verbal justifications analagous to "I wanted to" were also often given. However, when asked about the hypothetical dilemmas in stories, the children most frequently gave hedonistic reasons—justifications for behavior with reference to the expected gain for the self. They rarely talked of the needs of the other. Why should there be this difference between the children's discussion of hypothetical dilemmas and their explanations for their own sharing behavior? Eisenberg points out that, in the naturally occurring incidents in the nursery school, the explanations the children gave concerned relatively trivial actions of sharing or help (comforting was very rare). The actions were, that is, of little cost to the children. Moreover, they were asked for explanations after the incidents: if there had been some moral conflict for the child, involving self-interest, it had already been resolved. The children were not questioned about those incidents in which they had *not* acted in a prosocial way: presumably a much more self-interested justification for action might have been given then.

In the storybook task, in contrast, children were faced with situations that involved high costs for the individuals concerned. They were thus likely to consider seriously the matter of benefits to self. They also reasoned about decisions *not* to help others. It is therefore not surprising, Eisenberg argues, that here the children more frequently gave self-interested reasons than in their explanations for their already completed and often trivial helping actions in the nursery school.

Several important points stand out from these studies. First, frequency of spontaneous sharing observed in the nursery was related to the nature of the children's moral reasoning about the storybook situations. Children who shared a lot at nursery school were likely to offer judgments in terms of others' needs, and less likely to use hedonistic reasoning than the children who shared less often. But a second finding was that spontaneous *helping* was unrelated to moral reasoning. Rather, it was linked to sociability—a finding consistent with other evidence that helping is frequently used by children in group situations (and indeed at home) as a way of initiating play with another. It is clearly important to consider separately the different kinds of helpful and sharing actions, and to examine the costs involved for the child in each, before concluding that global measures of prosocial behavior always reflect altruistic motives.

Finally, the finding that children explained their own sharing behavior primarily in terms of the needs of others, and that sharing was correlated with moral reasoning in terms of others' needs in the judgment task, suggest this conclusion:

It is logical to suggest that preschoolers' references to others' needs when justifying prosocial acts represent a primitive empathic orientation. Such an empathic concern was often conveyed to the experimenter via the child's nonverbal behavior and tone of voice. In brief, empathic concerns appeared to frequently motivate the child's prosocial behavior. (Eisenberg and Neal, 1979, p. 229)

So children at nursery school do, it seems, *share* with others because of a concern for their needs—even though they apparently offer *help* more in order to engage in play with others than because of empathic concern. By four years old, children recognize the needs and wants of other children at school; they very much enjoy social exchange, and sharing with their friends and peers is apparently a pleasurable activity, not an act of sacrifice. (Recall the considerateness of Sarah in the quotation from Blum.) In contrast, sharing with a sibling appears to be less enjoyable for many children.

In summary, observations of responses to distress demonstrate that, early in the second year, children are interested in and often concerned about the distress of their siblings and mothers. By the second half of the second year, their recognition of the other's distress is clear, and the observations show that the children are capable of making sympathetic attempts to comfort their siblings and parents. In the third year, children are responding not only to overt displays of emotion but also to conditions of unhappiness or need, displaying a grasp of what would make a particular other person happier. The capacity to comfort or to show considerateness is sometimes, but by no means always, put into practice; whether the children do make attempts to alleviate the other's distress depends on the particular relationship and the context. In the second year, attempts to comfort are simple: most commonly they involve kissing, stroking, appeals to the mother. During the third year, they become more elaborate, reflecting quite a sophisticated grasp of how the other's distress might be alleviated—with distraction, affection, humor, or the aid of adults. The developmental changes show a growth from affective tuning, with relatively egocentric strategies of comfort to a comprehension of the different ways in which distressed feelings can be relieved.

Similarly, the evidence on sharing and helping shows that children by 18 months understand when their sibling wants what they have and on occasion will offer to share before they have been asked. Recall the evidence on disputes between siblings: by the third year, children not only recognize what the other wants but have grasped the idea that sharing is often expected (especially if it is food) and use this as one justification for their own demands. Older siblings help their younger siblings more than vice versa, and this difference might reflect changes in cognitive ability, in motivation, or in both. It seems likely that developments in cognitive and social abilities are important, whether or not there are also motivational changes. As with comforting, however, the motivation to help or share with a sibling is not high.

Self and self-interest

It is often argued that knowledge of others follows from or is modeled on inferences about the self. The point is clearly put by Thomas Hobbes in *Leviathan* (1561):

> they might learn truly to read one another, if they would take pains; that is *nosce te ipsum, read thyself* . . . for the similitude of the thoughts and passions of one man, to the thoughts and passions of another, whosoever looketh into himself, and considereth what he does, when he does *think, opine, reason, hope, fear,* &c. and upon what grounds; he shall thereby read and know, what are the thoughts and passions of all other men upon the like occasions.

That projection does in fact account for the understanding shown in much caring behavior is very much a matter of disputes among philosophers. And how far such a process is involved in the sympathetic responses of children in their second and third year is particularly unclear. It is argued that such projection requires a level of cognitive development beyond our one- and two-year-olds' capabilities, since it entails projecting oneself into another's situation, imagining what the self would feel and then assuming that the other feels similarly. Some have suggested, indeed, that two-year-olds' level of understanding others does not necessarily take the form of projection (Blum, 1987). But it is by no means evident how, if not by reference to self, the child begins to understand others' feelings. We are a long way from clarity here. Hoffman (1976) sees as significant the child's recognition of others as *similar* to the self, suggesting that this belief in similarity forms the basis for sympathy. Blum, by contrast, sees sympathy as not resting on perception of similarity but as prior to it.

We have no empirical grounds for assessing the relative support for these different views, although Blum's account (1987) raises an interesting point regarding self-concern. He argues in favor of a notion of identity formation that

> builds into it a sense of relatedness to others . . . the counterposition between "egoism" and "altruism," especially in philosophical discussion, suggests a kind of radical separation between self and others . . . The notion of altruism, for instance, conveys the implication that one's giving to others is entirely cut off from any concern for oneself, or even that it is at the expense of the self. In contrast to altruism, the notions, for example of "community" and "friendship" are relationships in which concern for others, while not reducible to self-interest, is not separable from concern for self. To be concerned for a friend, or for a community with which one closely identifies and is a member, is not to reach out to someone or something which is "wholly other" than oneself, but to that which shares a part of one's own self and is implicated in one's sense of one's own identity.

In this framework, then, the sympathetic concern shown by our two-year-olds does not conflict with an account of their developing social understanding in which concern for self plays a major role.

Note, too, that comforting actions shown to a parent did not appear to conflict with self-interest; with siblings as well, acts of comfort did not appear to involve self-sacrifice. Sharing with the sibling, however, often did involve self-sacrifice (to a parent the costs of such self-sacrifice might appear to be low, but the emotional behavior of the children indicated that giving up a toy to a *sibling* was a sacrifice that was by no means trivial). Although individual differences between children in their sharing behavior were marked, such acts were relatively infrequent in the group as a whole. In marked contrast was the children's eagerness to cooperate in joint activities and play with the sibling, and I turn to this next.

6

Cooperation between Siblings

A partner was absolutely essential to me if I was to bring my imaginary stories to life . . . In fact, I was always the one who expressed myself through them; I imposed them upon my sister, assigning her the minor roles which she accepted with complete docility . . . sometimes, spellbound by our play, we succeeded in taking off from the earth and leaving it far behind until an imperious voice suddenly brought us back to reality. Next day we would start all over again. We'll play *you know what,* we would whisper to each other as we prepared for bed.

—Simone de Beauvoir, *Memoirs of a Dutiful Daughter,* 1963

Very young children do not only fight, argue, and laugh at the misfortunes and misdeeds of others; they also cooperate with others in play at an astonishingly early age, and with an appreciation of the other's goals and mood that is impressive and delightful to observe. Their ability to cooperate in play with a sibling well before they are two years old far outstrips what might have been expected on the basis of studies of children in more formal settings or with less familiar companions (Dunn and Kendrick, 1982). It is an ability that depends on a sensitivity to the mood of the other, on a shared sense of the absurd and unexpected that presupposes a grasp of the expected, on a willingness to obey directions within the play context, to negotiate, concede to, and coordinate with another. And with the development of joint pretend play, it involves an intellectual leap into a shared world of pretend identities and roles.

In infancy, the play between mother and baby has been eloquently described, and its significance in the development of communication and emotional understanding is properly stressed. The development of babies' ability to take an active part in cooperative games such as peek-a-boo, hide-and-seek, or give-and-take, which involve sustained coordination between child and parent, is traced in a number of important studies (for instance, Bruner, 1977; Kaye, 1982; Stern, 1977; Trevarthen and Hubley, 1978). As they grow from 9 to 12 months, children take more responsibility for the particular part they play in such games and for turn taking (Ross, Goldman, and Hay, 1979). The infancy research establishes that by 12 months children can and do engage in games in the context of interaction with their mothers, where games are defined as two or more individuals working toward a mutual goal, with alternation of turns and repetitions of actions.

After these studies of infancy, there is relatively little systematic research into cooperation in play, until children reach the age of group life with other preschool children. One of the very few systematic studies of children with other family members is that of Dale Hay (1979), in which children of 12, 18, and 24 months were observed in a laboratory playroom with their parents and a set of standardized toys. The study clearly documents the increase in cooperative exchanges between 18 and 24 months. What happens in the more free-flowing family exchanges at home over this period?

In the years between early infancy and nursery school, play with a sibling demonstrates strikingly the young child's growing ability to cooperate in play, and in this chapter we look at six features of this cooperative play with a sibling that reflect the developmental changes in a child's growing social understanding.

Recognizing and sharing mood and action

From the earliest point at which we studied children in our Cambridge research, the children were observed to respond to the playful moods of their siblings, to laugh and frequently to join them by imitating their action. Indeed, in Study 4 (Dunn and Kendrick, 1982), such sensitivity to mood was observed in the secondborn baby siblings as early as 8 months old, as the following incidents illustrate.

1. Family F (Study 4). Child 8 months
Sibling bounces up and down, looking at C. Mutual
gaze. Child bounces up and down, while sibling continues to bounce. Both bounce together, laughing.

2. Family B (Study 4). Child 8 months
Sibling puts hand on highchair where C is sitting and
wiggles fingers on tray. Child watches. Sibling wiggles
fingers; both wiggle their fingers together, with mutual
gaze and laughter. Three minutes later C wigggles fingers
on tray, looks at sibling, and vocalizes.

The children's understanding of the sibling's play mood and
of the "script" of particular play sequences was evident in the
way they rapidly took up invitations by the older siblings—
invitations that were often very fleeting looks and smiles—and
themselves initiated repeats of such sequences.

3. Family C (Study 2). Child 18 months
Sibling runs his toy bike at C with "brmmmm" noise: C
laughs and runs away. C imitates sibling by picking up
construction toy and running it at sibling with "brmmm"
noise. Both run around room together, running their ve-
hicles and screaming with laughter. Sibling falls, C imitates fall with laughter. C offers sibling his hand, which
is covered with sleeve, and pulls him up. Both run
around room again, sibling dragging C by sleeve, both
laughing. C falls, sibling offers hand, in sleeve, C takes it,
and dragging game is repeated. Two minutes later C offers sleeve-covered hand; dragging game is repeated.

Sequences in which the children acted together, repeating
actions with excitement and laughter, were observed at every
stage of each of our studies. These rhythmic coaction sequences
involved a great range of actions: large-scale physical actions
(bouncing on sofa, dancing, jumping up and down, marching to
and fro, repeated falling down); waving, knocking, or tapping
objects; coordinated gestures; vocal rhythmic chanting or sing-

ing; and, in the third year, verbal chants or rituals. Peter and his older sister Sophie, the siblings in the next example, engaged in excited play of this sort on every occasion that they were observed, often for periods as long as forty minutes, and with a great deal of giggling.

4. Family W (Study 2). Child 24 months
Sibling enters room, looks at C and chants.

Sib: Loola Loola loola loola!
C (laughs and imitates): Loola loola loola loola!
Both chant together: Loola Loola loola loola!

Sibling picks up ribbon, walks (prancing) with it, chanting rhythmically. C watches, smiling, picks up another piece of ribbon and imitates prancing around room; both prance, chant, and laugh, waving ribbons. Sib climbs onto sofa and hangs upside down, still chanting. C imitates. Three minutes later sib hands C a piece of ribbon, starts chanting "Loola." C joins in chanting, both chant together. Four minutes later C takes another piece of ribbon, looks at sib and laughs. Sibling imitates by taking ribbon and laughs. Both climb onto cushion, waving ribbons and chanting.

It is striking that in these sequences very often both children express a great deal of positive excitement. I have discussed elsewhere the possible reasons why this might be—the enjoyment of acting together, the importance of the children's recognition of the other child as "like me" (Dunn and Kendrick, 1982). For the focus here on cooperation, it should be noted that sensitivity to another's positive mood and the ability to match that mood develop very early in human beings. Daniel Stern's demonstration of "affect attunement" between mothers and babies in the first year amplifies this point (1985). He argues that emotional resonance, "affect matching" or "affect contagion," "may well be a basic biological tendency among highly evolved social species, which becomes perfected in man" (p. 143).

Recognizing and cooperating in the other's goal

Cooperative actions in which children contribute to the other's play in a manner that reflects an understanding of the other's goals were observed with increasing frequency during the second year. Some children could already act in this cooperative way at 14 months.

5. Family B (Study 1). Child 14 months
Sibling begins to sing. C goes to toybox, searches, brings two toys to sibling, a music pipe and bells. Child holds out pipe to sibling and makes "blow" gesture with lips.

Later in the second year, unsolicited acts of helping in play were increasingly evident. By 18 months, thirty of the forty children were observed to act cooperatively in this way (and thirty-eight of the forty acted cooperatively when requested to do so by their sibling). Here are two typical examples of unsolicited help from 18-month-olds.

6. Family H (Study 1). Child 18 months
Sibling is playing game of running cars down a plastic track. C watches, runs to pick up car as it leaves track, brings it to sibling. Sibling runs car again, C again fetches it for him. Sequence repeated 4 times.

7. Family P (Study 2). Child 18 months
Sibling is acting out a fairy story with puppets. C watches, laughing. Goes to shelf and finds other puppets, appropriate to the play, and brings them to sibling.

The frequency of these unsolicited cooperative actions significantly increased between 18 and 24 months (Dunn and Munn, 1986). The two-year-olds acted cooperatively in about 7 percent of their interactions, and in a further 6 percent they joined cooperatively in pretend play with siblings. The comparable figures for their older siblings' cooperative actions at these observations were 13 percent and 11 percent of the interactions. Interestingly, the proportion of the children's cooperative exchanges with their siblings did not increase *further* between 24 and 36 months. Even though the children's skills of cooperating grew over this third year, it seems that their motivation to do so did not increase.

Compliance in the play context

In addition to these unsolicited contributions to the goals of others, children's ability and willingness to cooperate in play was evident in their compliance in the course of the play. Older siblings were frequently very managerial (if not dictatorial) in organizing play and in giving directions. Younger siblings did not always accept these orders but, given their resistance to sibling commands outside the play situation, their obedience within play was notable. This was especially so in pretend games, which in the early months depend heavily on the older sibling's setting up and maintaining the make-believe framework—but compliance was also shown in many other forms of play. The compliance of 21-month-old Ellie with her five-year-old brother's instructions means that she is an effective partner for him.

8. Family H (Study 1). Child 21 months
Sibling starts joint play sequence.

Sib to C: Look. Ellie. Let's get the hosepipe, Ellie. Let's get the hose pipe. (He fetches tube from vacuum cleaner.) Come on hosepipe. Ellie, can you help me with the hosepipe? (C helps him to carry tube.) Come on then, Ellie.
C: No!
Sib: Just pull this bit round. Come here. Pull that. (Child complies with instructions.)
Sib (pretending that water is coming out of tube): Shshshshsh!

C (imitates with appropriate noise and action): Shshshshsh!

Sib: Ellie. Now you put that to your ear. Oh ooh ooh! (Child complies with holding, calling, and listening. Two minutes later sibling starts variant of the game in which the vacuum tube is now a telephone.)

Sib: Hello! (C listens, then puts tube to her mouth and speaks, alternating listening and speaking appropriately for several turns.)

C: Hello! Hello!

Sib: Hello!

C: Hello.

Sib: Hello. Is anyone there?

C: Hello!

Sib: Hello! Hello goodbye!

M to C: Say byebye.

C to sib: Byebye.

One 18-month-old girl regularly cooperated in soccer games with her six-year-old brother, sequences that lasted between twenty and forty minutes, periods of concentrated play that are remarkably long for such a young child. A typical incident began with her watching him playing on his own with the ball. He then pointed to where she should stand and instructed her: "We're going to score." She repeatedly followed his instructions on where to stand, moving appropriately. He gave her the ball, helped her to kick it, shouted praise, and led her by the hand to where he wanted her to stand as goalie. When the ball bounced accidentally off her substantial tummy, he shouted praise again for saving the goal. When she picked up the goalpost and moved it (shades of the croquet game in Wonderland), he prohibited her gently and she complied immediately.

Reversal of roles

Increasingly often during the second and third year, there were sequences of play in which the children not only took one role in a joint game but were able to reverse roles. This was at first

at the sibling's suggestion, but toward the end of the second
year, the younger children took their own initiative. Thus the
child who was the chaser became the chased; the hider became
the seeker. The smoothness with which two-year-olds carried
out such role reversals illustrates how they could anticipate the
actions of the other and coordinate their own behavior. The
next example, in which Sally is first the one who hides and then
becomes the seeker, is typical of the 18-month-olds' reversal of
roles on instruction from an older sibling.

> 9. *Family T (Study 2). Child 18 months*
> C is listening to a story in which dog goes to hide; she
> runs to hide herself behind the curtain. Sibling follows
> and turns it into hide-and-seek game, pretending to look
> for her in the wrong place. Sibling says "Do it to me?"
> and C runs out to look for him.

Over the third year, the children's ability to cooperate in joint
activities with the sibling became increasingly effective. Most of
the cooperative actions by the younger child were still at 36
months suggested by the older sibling. For the forty families of
our second study, 65 percent of the 36-month-olds' cooperative
actions were suggested by the older sibling, and 35 percent were
unsolicited. But the successful way in which these unsolicited
actions were incorporated into the joint play reflects the effectiveness of the 36-month-old as a participant in the game: of the
children's unsolicited actions or suggestions, 77 percent were
taken up or accepted by the older sibling. The dominance of the
older sibling in joint activities is reflected in the comparable
figures for the firstborn: of their cooperative actions, 84 percent
were unsolicited, and only 16 percent were suggested by the
younger child.

But note that this success rate for cooperative actions is in
play in which both children are already engaged together with a
mutual goal. When the children came over and attempted to
help their siblings in activities in which the siblings had been
solely involved, their actions were much less welcome. At 36

months, 47 percent of such "helpful" actions were not accepted by the older sibling. The siblings' attempts to help the younger children in *their* solitary activities were slightly more successful: 22 percent were not accepted. In contrast, only 15 percent of the older siblings' suggestions or helpful actions made within cooperative activities were not accepted.

Cooperation in pretend

Perhaps the most striking feature of children's ability to cooperate in play during this transitional period is the ability to join in make-believe play. What such joint pretend play involves is the ability to share a pretend framework with another person, to carry out pretend actions in coordination with that other; it may also involve enacting the part of another person or thing, with the incorporation of another person into a reciprocal role (Miller and Garvey, 1981). In joint pretend play, then, we see not only the ability to coordinate and maintain a shared pretend framework but the mutual exploration of social rules and roles.

It is widely held that this is an advanced form of play, not shown until children are about three years old: "According to Piaget, pretend play is initially a solitary symbolic activity (Stage 1). Sociodramatic play (i.e., collective symbolism, Stage 2) does not begin until the latter part of the third year of life . . . Indirect evidence suggests that a shift from solitary to social pretense may occur at about 3 years of age" (Fein, 1981). But this account of the development of symbolic activity apparently reflects the way in which pretend play has been studied, rather than the way in which children's capacities actually develop. Joint pretend play has been almost exclusively studied in children over three, playing with peers. In one of the few studies that has looked at early role play at home in a family setting, Peggy Miller and Catherine Garvey (1984) described the development of play at "mothers and babies" between children and their mothers. Around 28 months, while their mothers provided support and tutoring, the children began to act as "mother" to a baby (doll), caring for the doll, and acting in a nurturing and affectionate manner. As the months went by, mothers continued to act as supportive spectators. Around 30 months, the children first referred to their own transformed identity, and at about 36 months they started to announce a reciprocal role. One girl explicitly announced herself as mother and assigned the role of baby to another child. Miller and Garvey distinguish this role play, in which the child adopts an identity other than the self and explicitly announces a transformed identity, from the earlier role enactment—in which the child's role identity can be inferred from speech and action. For a child to manage to transform her own identity into that of another, and to incorporate the partner into the joint pretend game, entails both understanding and considerable communicative skill.

In considering the development of social understanding and of cooperation in particular, pretend play highlights some especially interesting changes in a child's abilities. In the context of a warm and affectionate sibling relationship, some children manage extremely early to take part in joint pretend play. Such play demonstrates, first, their ability effortlessly to share a nonliteral framework; second, their ability to enact a role other than their own; third, their willingness to comply with the directions of the sibling; fourth, their ability to contribute innovations to that play; and fifth, their ability to play roles—to take on an identity other than their own and to coordinate the actions of this pretend person with those of another pretend person, played by the sibling.

The beginnings of these developments are seen as early as 18 months. Take this example from an observation of 18-month-old Mary, whose older sister Polly has set up a pretend birthday party with a cake, in the sand pit in the garden. Both children are singing "Happy Birthday"; in Mary's case the tune and the first two words are quite recognizable.

10. Family B (Study 1). Child 18 months

Sib: Dear Mary! You're three now.
C (nods): Mmm.

Sib: You can go to school now.

C *(nods):* Mmm.

Sib: Do you want to go to school now?

C: Mmm.

Sib: All right then. (Play voice) Hello Mary, I'm Mrs. Hunt. Do you want to help me do some of this birthday cake, do you? (Ordinary voice) We'd better do our birthday cake, hadn't we?

C *(sings appropriately):* "Happy birthday . . ." (Both children walk around garden, singing.)

Sib: We're at church now. We have to walk along. I'm like Mummy and you're like Baby. I'm Mummy. (Play voice) What, little one? We'd better go back to our birthday then.

C *(sings):* "Happy birthday . . ." (C holds hands up to sib to be carried.)

Sib: That's all right, little girl. Are you going to sleep?

Mary in this example enacts the role of a baby and behaves toward her sister as if Polly were the mother. In contrast to this baby behavior in the setting of the pretend game, she never once was observed to hold up her arms to be carried by her sister *out* of the context of pretend play, in the course of ten one-hour observations. According to the mother, this behavior was directed to her sibling only in the context of mother-baby games with the sibling as mother. Of the forty children in Study 2, six were, as 18-month-olds, instructed in joint pretend play in this manner by older siblings.

By 24 months, thirty-two of the forty secondborn children were observed to engage in joint pretend play, and the time spent in such play had increased significantly; by 36 months there was a further increase in frequency. Most interesting were the instances of joint role play in which the secondborn children demonstrated the ability to contribute to the pretend framework and that of taking on and explicitly announcing a new identity. Of our forty 24-month-olds, thirteen were observed to play in this way, announcing their identity as *driver,* as *daddy,* as *mummy,* as *baby,* as named characters, and so on. In the next example, the older sister explains to her mother that she is a particular railway engine, Henry, from a popular children's story. Her brother Martin, aged 24 months, listens and joins in by announcing his own identity as another of the engines from this favorite story—Gordon. The game continued for twenty minutes, with the engines driving all over the house, both chilren repeating their pretend identities. At one point the sister gave her brother some toothpaste and called him by his real name. He promptly corrected her, reiterating that he is *Gordon,* the engine.

11. Family C (Study 1). Child 24 months

Sib to M: There's the elephant. He's putting water all over this Henry. I'm Henry the train. The elephant's putting water all over I . . .

C: (laughs at sib) . . .

Sib: I'm being a train, Mum . . . I'm being a train. This train going very fast . . . I'm a train. Pushing the trucks . . .

C to sib: Beep beep. That's Gordon.

Sib to C: That's Gordon. I'm Henry the red one.

C: I'm Gordon.

Sib: Let's go . . . Oh Gordon's going the other way.

C: I'm Gordon.

Sib: Henry's a train. This Henry. This Henry's going to brush its teeth.

C: I'm Gordon. That's Gordon . . . I like Gordon.

Sib: I'm Henry the train. Are you following me, Gordon?

C: Yes.

Sib: And I'm Henry.

C: Yes.

Sib: Henry and you Gordon have both got to brush the teeth. Trains have to brush their teeth. (Game continues with sib giving running commentary on both their actions, referring to each of them as Henry and Gordon.)

Sib: Do you want to brush your teeth, Gordon?

C: Yes . . .

Sib: There you are, Martin.
C: I'm *Gordon.* (To observer) I'm Gordon.

In the great majority of incidents of joint pretend play that we observed in the second year, the older sibling was responsible for initially setting up the game and designating the roles to be taken, but in many instances the younger child did make some innovative contributions to the narrative. In the next example, the little girl is playing with her sister: in the course of a long, wandering pretend game, they pretend to go to bed and the little girl addresses her sister as Mummy—a new move in the fantasy—and later, when instructed to eat by her "Mummy," comments that she likes the food (a pencil).

12. Family M (Study 2). Child 24 months

Sib: We got to leave it there to go to sleep (leans back, sighs, shuts eyes). You sleep with me! (sighs and whispers).
C to observer: We're going to bed! (Sib sighs.) (To sib) What's the matter, Mummy?
Sib (whispers): Go to sleep.
C: Mummy? Mummy?
Sib: Yes. Go to sleep.
C: Mummy?
Sib: Yes?
C: Come here.
Sib (cuddles her): Yes. Have you got cold hands?
C: Yes.
Sib: Ooh! Rub it up that cold hands. (Pretend game continues for 11 turns.)
Sib: Do you want some dinner?
C: Want some dinner.
Sib: Have that dinner (gives her a pencil).
C (pretends to eat pencil): Yum yum. I like it. I like it.

The establishment and maintenance of joint play depends on both children's accepting or negotiating the other's contributions. Yet it is of course unclear exactly what the two-year-olds understand about the joint role game or about the identity transformations of themselves or their siblings in this play. On occasion the younger refused to obey the older's instructions and simply left the game. But the compliance that they usually showed to their siblings is striking, given their resistance to the sibling's commands in other nonplay circumstances. It is highly unlikely that the children would have obeyed the often fierce directions and prohibitions given by the sibling in the role of "mother" or "teacher" unless they recognized the nonliteral, playful nature of those commands. (For further analyses and discussion of siblings' joint pretend play, see Dunn and Dale, 1984.)

The influence of siblings and mothers

There is a striking difference between the joint pretend play of these children with their siblings and the play of the same children with their mothers. In the sequence of play with mother and child together, the mothers acted as spectators to the play, attentive and supportive, but rarely as active participants. They behaved, that is, just as the mothers in the study of Miller and Garvey (1984) behaved. In contrast, the sibling partners expected the children to coordinate their role play with their own, to follow their instructions, and to show evidence of their identity within the play role. A much higher degree of cooperation was demanded, and by and large it was given. The differences were strikingly significant. In 60 percent of sequences of play with child and sibling together, the sibling and child acted together as *complementary actors*. In contrast, mothers acted in this way in only 15 percent of the sequences of pretend play in which they joined the children. In 85 percent they acted as *spectators,* and the joint game required no coordinated participation between the two partners (Dunn and Dale, 1984).

This distinction between role of mother and role of sibling in the development of young children's ability to participate in joint make-believe is brought out, too, in the analyses of individual differences between children in their cooperative behavior. First, there are substantial correlations between the cooperative behavior of the older sibling and that of the younger sibling at any one time point. For instance, in Study 3 there were correlations of $r(40) = 0.75$ between the 36-month-old children's cooperative actions within pretend play and those of their siblings. Even more striking was the correlation between their cooperative actions in other contexts and those of their sibling: $r(40) = 0.90$. The correlations between the siblings' cooperative behavior are also significant *over time.* Thus in families in which the firstborn sibling frequently acted cooperatively toward the 18-month-old secondborn, six months later the secondborn were more likely to act cooperatively than the children whose older siblings had rarely acted cooperatively: $r(40) = 0.63$.

Second, the evidence from two separate studies shows that in families in which there is a friendly affectionate relationship between siblings, as reflected in other features of their behavior, the younger children become active and cooperative in joint pretend play. Thus in the forty families of Study 2, children whose relationship with their siblings as 18-month-olds was characterized by low frequencies of sibling teasing and of child distress or anger in conflict with the sibling were, as 36-month-olds, more frequently cooperative than children whose relationships with their siblings were less harmonious—$r(40) = 0.31$ and 0.30 respectively. Similarly, in Naomi Dale's (1983) study of 24-month-olds, children whose relationships with their siblings were, by other criteria, *very friendly,* engaged in joint pretend play more than five times as much as children whose relationship with their sibling was *somewhat friendly,* and ten times more than those whose relationships was categorized as *unfriendly.* In contrast to these connections between the behavior of the older sibling and the cooperative behavior of young secondborn children, no significant correlations were found between mothers' behavior toward their children and the participation of the children in joint pretend with the sibling at this early age.

Development of negotiation

During the third year, the children's ability to contribute to the joint pretend play rapidly increased. So too did their ability to contest and negotiate about the course of the pretend play. Let us look at the innovations and negotiations made by a girl of 30 months, Annie, in a game of mother-and-babies that was initiated by Carol, her older sister, with a command to Annie to "pretend you're a baby or my mummy." It is a sequence that was by no means unusual in complexity or length; it lasted for 140 conversational turns, and Annie made several contributions to the play narrative. She also acted both compliantly and non-compliantly:

14. *Family A (Study 3). Child 30 months*
C's innovations in joint pretend play, for her role as Baby:
   Makes babbling noises.
   Crawls.
   Says she can't put slippers on: "I'm baby."
   Designates "baby bed."
   Asks for porridge.
   Plays guitar in a way she designates as "a babby
      way . . . Me babby."
   Addresses sibling as "Mummy."
   Acts naughty with guitar.
   Pretends to get lost.
   Snores.
   In answer to sibling asking why she is crying ("What's
      wrong babbu?") replies "Me can't get to sleep."
   Instructs sibling on what she should say, as Mummy.
C's disputes and noncompliance with sibling over course of pretend play:
   When told to babble and not to cry, cries.
   Criticizes sibling's action in terms of role: "No you not
      a baby."
   Denies that what she is drinking (pretend) is a milk-
      shake.

Denies that they are both tired in the game.
Refuses to go on "Mummy's" knee.
C's compliance with sibling's actions or suggestions dur-
ing the play:
   Sibling says go to sleep; C complies, pretends to sleep.
   Sibling gives "drink"; C drinks it.
   Sibling gives "food"; C eats it.

It is clear that by 30 months this little girl is far more than a
submissive partner, obeying her sister's commands—she is a
highly active participant in the play, disputing several of the
sibling's suggestions and making many innovative contributions.

For the sample of forty families, the data on children's cooperation in pretend play show that, of the cooperative actions
performed at 36 months, 62 percent were following the instructions of the older sibling and 38 percent were innovations of the
younger child. These pretend innovations were largely successful: 73 percent were taken up or responded to positively by the
older sibling. The older siblings still tended to play a dominating
role in the structure of the play as a whole. The comparable
figures for the older siblings show that, of the cooperative actions of the sibling, 70 percent were innovative, and the younger
siblings responded very cooperatively to these. Only 10 percent
were not accepted. Of the siblings' cooperative actions, 30 percent were suggested or solicited by the younger child at 36
months. In those families that engaged in joint pretend play—
thirty-three of the forty families at 36 months—both younger
and older sibling cooperated effectively.

In their second and third years, these children showed themselves to be willing cooperators in play, picking up the mood of
the sibling, coordinating their own actions to those of the sibling, taking roles complementary to those of the sibling, and by
two years old sharing the collective symbolism of a pretend
world. In the context of play, the children *helped* toward achieving a mutual goal. Note, however, that this evidence for coop-

eration and aid does not conflict with the argument that self-concern is an important motivating force in a child's development. The play of the older sibling was rivetingly interesting for these children; the skills that the younger child was just developing were effortlessly and smoothly demonstrated by the older—and their play acted as a magnet to draw the attention of the younger. It was in the interest of the younger children to participate in such play, and when the game lacked appeal, they quickly stopped cooperating. Yet what stands out from these observations is the delight with which the children explored social roles and rules—hardly the behavior of children exclusively centered on their own narrow vision of the world. Their increasing interest in how and why people behave as they do, and in the ways of the world, is evident not only in children's pretend games but in their conversations and questions during the third year, the subject of the next chapter.

7

Talking about Others: Questions, Interventions, Narrative

Interest in other people—both children and adults—was a characteristic feature of most of the children in the study, and manifested itself in many different topics: their friends, other members of the family, growing up, birth, illness and death, what people did for their living, and so on. Indeed, it is worth remarking on the breadth of the children's interests, and the complexity of the issues that they raised. It is sometimes supposed that children of this age have special childish interests, mainly to do with mothers, babies, dolls, teddies and animals, and such a view would be reinforced by most of the picture books published for children of this age. The conversations in our study suggest that, on the contrary, all human experience was grist to their intellectual mill.

—Barbara Tizard and Martin Hughes, *Young Children Learning*, 1984

The children described by Tizard and Hughes in this quotation were just four years old when their conversations at home were studied. By this age, children show a remarkable breadth of interest in their social world and a coherent grasp of the bases of human action in terms of beliefs, intentions, and desires. They can—and do—talk about intentions, motivation, and false beliefs; they distinguish intended acts from mistakes (Schulz, 1980) and judge correctly how an actor will act, given mistaken beliefs (Perner, Leekham, and Wimmer, 1987). In experimental settings they show that they can grasp the psychological causality determining the actions of storybook characters in terms of the goals and beliefs of those actors (Nezworski, Stein, and Trabasso, 1987). They pursue with persistence inquiries about why people act in the way they do. How and when does this explicit verbal interest and understanding of others develop? The coherence of three-year-olds' causal understanding of the bases of human action has been demonstrated by Wellman (1986); yet the examples he cites are cases in which the child demonstrates his grasp of the causal bases of his *own* actions. On the early development of children's understanding of the causes of others' actions, we have very little information. What is it about other people and the social world that excites young children's interest and curiosity, and how is their growing understanding linked to the developments in their social relationships?

Important findings on these questions come from the study of children's early causal statements and questions by Lois Hood and Lois Bloom (1979). It was psychological rather than physical causality that interested the two- and three-year-old children in that study. They discussed motivation and intention, and Hood and Bloom emphasize that there was a gradual change in orientation from expressing causal relations in connection with their *own* intentions toward referring both to their own and to other peoples' actions and intentions. "Development proceeded from talking about actions of self and others as expression of what the child has in mind to the beginning of the ability to inquire into the contents of mind in others with *Why?* questions" (Bloom and Capatides, 1987). Over the third year the children were learning, they suggest, to take into account the activities of people other than themselves in their causal statements, but reference to the other person usually took the form of directives, in which the children attempted to get the listener to do something for them.

The strategy employed in our Cambridge studies was to look not specifically at causal references about self and other, but more generally at the children's comments and questions about other people. What we found suggested a picture of children's interest in others that complements the findings of Bloom and her colleagues. It was a pattern that changed during the third year, and there were important developments in the children's participation as family members that paralleled the changes in their talk about others. These crucial developments in the ability to reflect on and ask about the behavior of others affect children's relationships in myriad ways and are evident in many different aspects of their talk. I will trace the developments here in just three features of the children's conversations: first, their comments and inquiries about others, and the context in which these comments were made; next, their interventions in the conversations of others; finally, their narratives about others.

Comments and questions about others

The children in our studies talked with increasing frequency about other people from 18 months on: their whereabouts, feelings, actions and the reasons for those actions, transgressions, and mistakes. The pattern of this interest changed during the second and third year. At 24 months their comments and questions focused chiefly on whereabouts and actions, but increasingly during the third year they talked and asked about feeling states, about how rules applied to others; after 28–30 months they commented on the mental states of others (thinking, knowing, remembering, believing). An analysis of the questions they asked about other people illustrates these changes.

Questions

In Fig. 7.1 the inquiries that the six children in Study 3 made about other people are grouped into four general classes—inquiries about where they are, about what they are doing and why (excluding queries about forbidden behavior), about what desires they have or what feeling state they are in and why, and finally about forbidden behavior, obligation, and how rules apply to others. We see that initially the children's questions are mostly concerned with others' actions and their whereabouts, but the proportion of their queries about the feelings and wants of others increases, and so too does the proportion of their questions about how social rules are applied and how people break them. The figure also shows the data from the forty

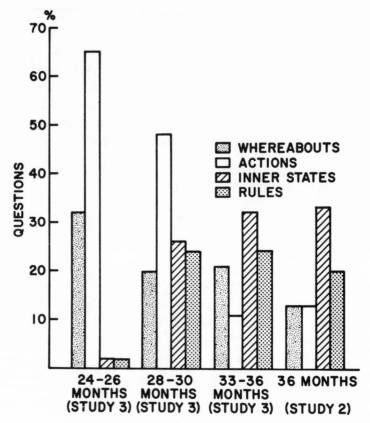

Fig. 7.1 Questions about other people (Studies 2 and 3)

children of Study 2 at 36 months: the proportion of questions about others that fall into the four categories are quite similar to those of the children of Study 3 at 33–36 months—which provides some reassurance that the data for our six children are reasonably representative. The changes in the *frequencies* of inquiries show a similar pattern.

The nature and context of these questions varied widely. Questions about the whereabouts of others were on occasion apparently motivated by mild anxiety: "Where's Mummy?" was occasionally asked if the mother was in another room. But most of the questions about whereabouts concerned others in the child's world who were not expected to be in the home at that time, and they were certainly not anxious. The interest of the children in knowing where their friends and family members were, and what they were doing, was evident, as was their pleasure in recounting with the mother the familiar routines these other people follow. For at 24 and 26 months, such questions often formed part of a familiar series of questions, and if they were not answered, the children themselves often furnished the answer, as the next example illustrates.

1. Family J (Study 3). Child 24 months

C: Where Glynnis gone? Where Glynnis gone? Where Glynnis gone? Pick Maria up. Pick Maria up. Pick Maria up. Here Glynnis gone work (repeated 3 times). Glynnis gone work. Derek gone work. Daddy gone work.

In our study of the arrival of a sibling, Study 4, similar sequences of questions from the firstborn children were also recorded.

2. Family S (Study 4). Child 24 months

C: Aunty Phil?
M: Aunty Phil's at work.
C: Sal?
M: Sal's at school.
C: Sal?
M: Sally's at school.
C: Marie?
M: With Marie, yes.
C: Come school?
M: You can't go to school. You're not big enough, are you? You got to get a bit bigger to go to school.

3. Family P (Study 4). Child 26 months

C: Where's Ken gone? Where's Ken gone?
M: He's at work.

C: Work. On bike.
M: Yeah. Gone on his bike.
C: Bus and bike. Where's Grandad?
M: Oh he's at work too.
C: Where's Uncle Liz?
M: *Aunty* Liz.
C: Aunty Liz?
M: She'll be at work as well.

Questions about people's actions were often about the mother's or sibling's actions there and then, focused on the immediate present. Thus Mike at 30 months, watching his mother icing a cake, asks her: "Mum, what you doing? What you doing, Mum? Icing that?" And at 36 months, again watching her cook, he asks: "Why doing that on the pastry? . . . Have to squeeze it out do another one, won't you?" Such inquiries became over the course of the year increasingly explicit attempts to clarify why someone was acting in a particular way. Both Cathy and Polly were asking such *why* questions as early as 26 months. When Polly's mother was helping her older sibling to put up pictures, she asked "Why Mummy sticking a drawing?" Sometimes these questions appeared to be attempts to make sense of social behavior the child did not understand. Thus Jay at 33 months asked his mother, "What say 'Ah-uhh!' for?" and at 36 months asked, "Why did you say 'What's that?'?"

Two features of these questions about peoples' actions stand out. First, the children's interest in mistakes, in people who are in trouble, or in odd and unexpected behavior was very clear. The mildest expression of annoyance or exclamation at errors produced inquiries about the cause of the comment. Thus Kerry at 26 months, when her mother exclaims "Aah!" as she spills something, asks "What you done? You haven't——?" And at 36 months, when her mother exclaims "Ooh!" she asks, "Why? You o.k.?" Jay at 30 months asks about the unusual circumstances of his father's going to bed in the daytime and, receiving no answer, goes on at some length to supply an explanation himself: "Why Daddy gone a bed for a minute? Where he? . . .

He gone a bed for a minute. He got cold. Him got cold. No, Daddy got cold. Him gone in a bed. He has. He got——gone a bed for a minute."

Inquiries about actions often followed quickly upon comments that other family members were cross, lazy, or in trouble. Thus Kerry at 26 months, hearing about potential trouble, asks about her mother's action and repeats the question.

4. Family S (Study 3). Child 26 months

M: If I don't iron some of Daddy's shirts I shall be in a row tomorrow.
C: Why do?
M: ——
C: Why you iron?
M: Take the creases out.
C: Oh.

Mistakes made by others were often asked about with interest, and this curiosity was sometimes focused upon the observer, as in 28-month-old Polly's interest in the observer's comment that she forgot her pen.

5. Family C (Study 3). Child 28 months

C *to observer:* You forgot your pen. Forgot your pen . . . could——the other pen. Did you couldn't find your pen at home?

The second striking feature of these questions about actions concerns their pragmatic context. As the examples above show, most of these inquiries about others' actions were disinterested, in the sense that the children were not pressing for their own immediate wishes or attempting to get others to do something. The questions asked by our six children about other people seemed to be active attempts to make sense of the world rather than to meet immediate needs. (Tizard and Hughes found that two-thirds of the questions their four-year-olds asked were of this sort.)

Such disinterested curiosity about others' actions was often evident in the context of stories read to the child, when the children attempted to clarify the basis of actions by storybook characters. In the next example, Polly is puzzling over the actions of a rabbit (who is both talking and attempting to catch a bus). She herself offers a gloss on the rabbit's reaction to missing the bus.

6. *Family P (Study 3). Child 36 months*
M is reading story and quotes rabbit as saying "Wait for me!"

C: Why saying wait for me?
M: Catching the bus.
C: And it does annoy rabbit he don't got the bus.

Sometimes these inquiries about the actions of storybook characters developed into an extended series of questions, as the children puzzled over behavior they didn't understand. Annie in the next example is only 26 months old, but her attempts to understand the behavior of the character in the book her mother is reading parallel the "passages of intellectual search" that Tizard and Hughes describe in four-year-olds talking with their mothers.

7. *Family A (Study 3). Child 26 months*

C *(referring to character in story):* Why is he putting all the shopping away?
M: Why?
C: Mmm.
M: So that it's not all over the place. All on the sides and the floor. He puts it all in the cupboards.
C: Why did he put it all——put it all in the cupboards?
M: What did you just say?

C: Why did he put it——?

M: Why?

C: Yeah.

M: 'Cos if you don't put all in the cupboard, where's it going to go?

C: Don't know.

M: Can't have——

C: In a shopping bag.

M: You can't leave it in the shopping bag, can you? You'll be tripping over the shopping bags.

C: You won't.

M: You will! If we leave it in the shopping bags, what are we going to put in the shopping bags?

Questions about rules, obligations, and forbidden behavior

The proportion of questions about the application of rules to others and forbidden behavior increased, as Fig. 7.1 shows, toward the end of the third year, but such curiosity about how rules apply to others was apparent earlier. In the next example Jay is told by his older brother that he is not allowed to have knives near his face, and he asks about who else this rule applies to.

8. Family J (Study 3). Child 30 months

Sib to C: You're not allowed to put knives in your face.

C: Just you?

Sib to C: No. Not me.

C: Glynnis?

Sib to C: No. Not anybody.

And it will come as no surprise to parents that discussion of intended forbidden actions by others—conspiracy over deviance—forms a context of eager questions to the sibling. Jan's older brother announces that he is going to pee in the garden, a forbidden act, and she fastens on it with delight.

9. *Family L (Study 2). Child 36 months*

C: Are you going to do a wee wee? Are you? All right? Are you going to do it here? Shall I do mine?

Questions about feelings, perceptions, and inner states

Questions about other peoples' feelings, perceptions, and mental states increased, both in frequency and proportion, over the third year (Fig. 7.1). The nature of these inquiries varied greatly, as did their context—a point to which I shall return. It is important here to note that the children engaged in conversations about feeling states even when their ability to talk explicitly about feelings or actions was very limited. By 24–25 months, conversations about feeling states were relatively frequent in two separate samples of children: the forty secondborn children from Study 2 and sixteen of the firstborn children from Study 4. Further, the interest of the children was in these conversations by no means exclusively focused on themselves. The proportion of conversational turns about feelings that concerned others was 40 percent in the forty children of Study 2, and in the sixteen firstborn children from Study 4 observed at 25 and 32 months of age, it was 60 percent and 50 percent respectively (Dunn, Bretherton, and Munn, 1987). We examined in detail these conversations about feeling states during the second and third year, and the analysis showed that the children were not simply referring to feeling states in a routine way to keep the conversation going.

For instance, they were interested in the causes of feeling states. They asked about antecedents and on occasion offered causal explanations. We have seen in the chapters on conflict and benevolence that children have a firm grasp of the links between actions and harm to others; thus we should not be surprised that they also commented on causes of warmth, cold, fear, tiredness, anger, and annoyance in others (rabbits missing buses included). Sometimes these conversations revealed a persistent attempt to get to the bottom of what caused the other person's state—as in the next example where Jay overhears his mother telling the observer about a dead mouse that frightens her.

10. *Family J (Study 3). Child 28 months*

C: What's that frighten you, Mum?
M: Nothing.
C: What's that frighten you?
M: Nothing.
C: What is it? . . . What's that down there, Mummy? That frighten you.
M: Nothing.
C: That not frighten you?
M: No. Didn't frighten me.
C: What that there?

The children used their references to feeling states for a variety of practical purposes: to influence others' behavior, to explain their own, and to gain clarification about the behavior of others. In Study 2, around 50 percent of the references to feeling states by the forty children were attempts to change or guide others' behavior or to explain their own feelings. However, inquiries about *other peoples'* feelings were commonly not linked to an immediate goal or need of the child. Such questions were most frequently either about others who were hurt or upset—"Are you all right?" "Why you crying?"—or about another person's likes or dislikes, and these were rarely tied to a desire of the child. Lively curiosity, for instance, was shown in the observer's likes, dislikes, and feelings. The questions addressed to her in Study 3 included "Do you like monsters?" "Do you like dogs?" "Want a little bit of biscuit?" "Do you get cross?" "You like your baby?"

Self-orientation or disinterested curiosity?

The suggestion that many of the children's questions about other people were not closely tied to their own immediate needs raises the question of whether during the third year there is a decrease in the self-interest or self-orientation that is so noticeable in other aspects of the children's behavior. To explore this possibility we first consider the context of references to others, both comments and questions, and then the children's interventions in others' conversations.

The children's references to other people were categorized according to whether they occurred in a context in which the children were (a) teasing, (b) in dispute, (c) drawing attention to their own interests, (d) in joint play with another, (e) making narrative comments in solo play, (f) drawing attention to the transgression of others, (g) expressing concern about the state of others, (h) commenting on how social rules applied to others, (i) commenting on the behavior of others (other than transgressions). The first five of these categories could be considered as self-oriented, while the remaining categories are disinterested in orientation.

Did the proportion of these two broad groupings of the comments about others, self-oriented versus disinterested, change in the course of the third year? Our analysis showed that while for each of the six children in Study 3 the frequency and proportion of disinterested comments increased between 24 and 26 months, there was no further increase in the proportion over the course of the third year as a whole. That is, although there are striking developments in children's ability to discuss the inner states of others, the cause of their feelings, and the application of social rules to those others, there was between 26 and 36 months *no decrease* in the children's self-orientation. Their talk about others was just as likely to be related to their own interests at 36 months as it had been at 26 months.

Interventions in the conversation of others

Another quite different approach to the issue of the children's interest in others and their self-orientation was through an analysis of their interventions in the conversation between other people. A great deal of the talk that goes on within a family is not directed at the two-year-old, especially if there are older siblings about. To begin to participate successfully in these family conversations, children must be able to tune in to the topic of conversations that are neither directed to them nor necessarily focused upon their interests or needs; they must be able to make interventions that are relevant to the others' topics of interest, and—if they are to be effective conversationalists— they must be able to add new information to the conversation. Effective intervention then would present considerable difficulties to a child who is insensitive to the interests of others. He might well interrupt others' talk, but how well would he manage to join conversations by adding contributions relevant to the previous topic?

Our analyses (described in full in Dunn and Shatz, 1988) showed, first, that such interventions were frequent for each of the children studied. On average, 22 percent of the children's conversational turns during the third year were interventions in the talk of others. The rate of intervention increased over the year: at 24 months they intervened on average twelve times per one hundred opportunities to intervene, and by 36 months this rate of intervening had doubled to more than twenty-five times per one hundred opportunities.

In some of these interventions, the children showed sensitivity to the topic of the others' conversation and made a relevant contribution. In the next example, 28-month-old Polly intervenes three times in the conversation between her older sister and mother, which is about her sister's pretend game of shopping at Sainsbury's, a grocery store. Her first two interventions (labeled 1 and 2) are focused on her sister's needs in the game and are helpful; her third is more typical in its self-orientation.

11. Family C (Study 3). Child 28 months
M and sibling discussing sibling's projected pretend shopping trip. C interrupts with suggestion.

C to sib: Better get your cheque book. (1)
Sib: Yes . . .

Sib to M (later in pretend game): Did I leave my bag there?
M to S: You didn't leave your bag at Sainsbury's, did you?
Sib to M: What I want?
C to sib (points out mislaid bag): No, at home! (2)
M to S: You left it at home! . . .
Sib to M (confused about having lost her list and her bag):
    Umm——what did I want then?
M to sib: What did you want?
C (triumphantly): I got all my shopping list in. I's got my
    shopping list in my bag. (3)

Not only did the children's rate of intervention increase during the third year, but the likelihood that they would add new
information when intervening also increased, from a median
proportion of 39 percent (new to total information) at 24
months to 68 percent (new to total information) at 36 months.
Indeed, they were far more likely to add new information when
intervening in others' conversations than when they themselves
were directly addressed.

Whether or not these interventions were relevant to the talk
that preceded them depended crucially upon the topic of that
conversation. If the others were talking about the child himself,
then he was extremely likely to join the conversation with a
comment that was relevant, even at 24 months: 95 percent of
such interventions were relevant. But if the previous topic was
someone or something other than the child, the children were
much less likely to make a pertinent intervention; in such cases
they were most likely to talk about themselves. Of the interventions in others' conversations focused on the topic of someone
else, 68 percent were contributions in which the children talked
about themselves, as Polly did in her third intervention in example 11. There was no decrease over the third year in this propensity to turn talk-about-others to talk-about-self. There was,
however, a developmental change in the nature of such attempts
to turn the family conversation from the topic of other people to
themselves. At the beginning of the third year, such interventions
were more likely to be irrelevant than relevant, with a median of

only 21 percent relevant at 24 months. But through the third year, there was an increasing probability that such other-to-self interventions would be relevant. Thus by 36 months the proportion of incidents in which the interlocutors were talking about others, and the child intervened by turning the topic to self with a relevant intervention, was as high as 47 percent.

In other words, the children remained as self-oriented at 36 months as they had been at 24 months, in the sense that they were just as concerned to turn conversations about others to conversations about themselves. But they became more adept at intervening to turn the focus of the talk to the topic of themselves *in a relevant fashion*. Incidentally, this turning of topic-of-other to topic-of-self was just as evident in the children's talk when they were addressed directly. Indeed, the topic of self remained of paramount interest to the children throughout the year, and there was no significant change in the proportion of total conversational turns that were about self. At 36 months the median proportion was 59 percent (range 46–67 percent).

In summary, the children showed themselves increasingly effective in intervening in family conversations through the third year. This effectiveness reflected their attention to the talk of others, although they used this ability to turn the talk to that absorbing topic—themselves and their own interests.

Narrative

> My feelings were very acute; they used to amuse themselves by making me cry at sad songs and dismal stories. I remember "Death and the Lady", "Billy Pringle's Pig", "The children sliding on the ice all on a summer's day", and Witherington fighting on his stumps at Chevy Chase. This was at two years old, when my recollection begins—prior identity I have none—They tell me I used to beg them not to proceed. (Robert Southey, letter to G.C. Bedford, 30 September 1796)

The power of narrative to hold children's interest is evident from early in the second year. By two years old, as many parents know, children are frequently excited and moved by stories.

Southey's reminiscences show the power of these early experiences of narratives about others, especially narratives about sad feelings and disasters. And this fascination with narrative is a striking feature of children's talk about other people. From the time they first begin to talk, children's interest in the story of what happened is clear. It is evident in their enjoyment of parent-and-child conversations about events in their own life—yesterday, last Christmas, at the seaside in the summer; it is evident in their absorption in storybooks; and, most strikingly, it is evident in their own narratives as they play, alone or with others.

This sensitivity to narrative is both intriguing and deeply instructive. Persuasive arguments have been made that we account for our own actions and for the way others act principally in terms of narrative, story, or drama. In children's absorbed interest in narrative, we see how powerful narrative images are in generating a particular self in a particular culture: "Stories define the range of anatomical characters, the settings in which they operate, the actions that are permissible and comprehensible. And thereby they provide, so to speak, a map of possible worlds in which action, thought, and self-definition are permissible (and desirable)" (Bruner, 1986, p. 66). In the child's enthusiasm for narrative we see a readiness to explore and understand the social world, a readiness that is not taught, although it may be fostered and enjoyed by others. Children's interest in stories about themselves is not perhaps surprising, but why should they be so fascinated by the history of another person's encounters?

To explore the question of what it is that interests children in narrative about others, we examined the narratives that the six children of Study 3 told about others in their conversation, in their play, and as stories were read to them. A narrative was defined according to Umiker-Sebeok (1977), as a description of one or more events that will inform the addressee that "something happened" (see Appendix 2). We included narratives about future events (see examples 13 and 14 below; also Miller and Sperry, 1987).

The results show that, in the course of the third year, there is a development in children's narratives about others that parallels the changes in their questions about others. At 24–26 months, the narrative comments on others in stories or in solo play were too infrequent to permit detailed analysis. But increasingly from 28 months on, the children made narrative comments on others. Between 26 and 30 months, the numbers of narratives increased from seventeen (26 months) to thirty-six (28 months) to ninety (30 months). Some of these narratives included several comments or "clauses," in the terminology of Labov and Waletzky (1967).

Fig. 7.2 shows that the proportion of narratives about others' forbidden actions and rule breaking and about the feeling states of others increased in the last few months of the third year. The figure also shows the data from the forty children of Study 2 at

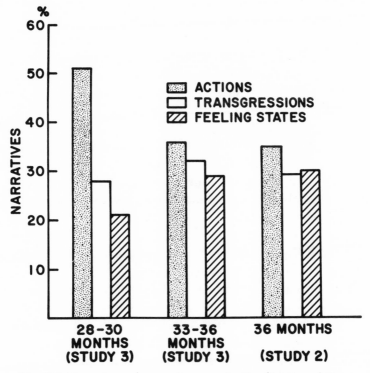

Fig. 7.2 Narratives about other people (Studies 2 and 3)

36 months, with a pattern of the proportion of narrative comments about others that is very similar to that of the six children
of Study 3. The solo fantasy games that the children played with
their toys and dolls frequently involved, for instance, narratives
that included the toy characters behaving in a forbidden way. The
following incidents from the transcripts of the six children at 33
months are typical: Polly played a game in which a group of toys
went off on the train, wanted to go to the toilet, and all proceeded
to "do a wee" in forbidden places—not once but repeatedly; Jay's
teddy went to sleep, woke up, spilled his drink, went to sleep
again, was smacked; Kerry played a game with a naughty snake
and a doll that had a dirty bottom ("naughty naughty bottom
girl"); Cathy's teddy was naughty, repeatedly. Accidents leading
to people being in distress were also common themes, as the
following example from 36-month-old Ben illustrates.

12. Family T (Study 2). Child 36 months
Child playing with figures who are at a fair.

C: And then this man has a ride. So does this other man.
   Shoogabashicks. Shoogabashicks. One falls off . . . And
   they both fall off and cry.

Such dramas are familiar stuff to play therapists. Whether or
not we choose to view these fantasies as expressions of the
children's need to act out inner feelings of disturbance or aggression, we should not ignore the evidence they provide on
which aspects of social behavior are of significance to the children. Their comments while watching television show the same
pattern of interest in naughty actions, in accidents, and in the
feeling states of the characters.

What this pattern of findings shows is an increase in narrative
comments about others that coincides with the appearance of
comments on others' mental states and with questions about
others' feeling states, the causes of their behavior, and the application of social rules to others. It is a developmental pattern
that also coincides with the transitions that Hood and Bloom

describe in their study of children's causal understanding: first a transition from causal statements to answering causal questions, then a transition to asking such causal questions themselves. It suggests that a new curiosity about others is born with the development of the ability to refer to and reflect upon other minds. As the children's ideas about others and the social world become clearer, they develop more elaborate theories about that world. It follows that there are more issues to clarify—with questions—as well as more possibilities for play.

The basis for children's interest in narrative is their interest in human events. The significance of this remarkable development can be seen in many different domains of their behavior, any or all of which we might choose to stress. We could emphasize narrative as a forum in which cultural guidance and teaching occurs and in which the child develops a new sense of self-within-culture, as Bruner argues. We could also stress the importance of these new skills of narrative in the pragmatics of children's social relationships. In their handling of disputes, they can now explain that it was the sibling's fault that something happened; in trouble with their mothers, they can now extricate themselves by recounting a sequence of their own and others' actions; in the sharing of exciting experiences and jokes about a story of what happened to another, there is a new dimension to their intimacy with others.

Most important, children now have new abilities to get others to attend to what interests *them*. While in the second year their determination to get others to pay attention was expressed clumsily with gesture, vocalization, and talk that was often, inevitably, misunderstood, their newfound narrative skills in the third year give them far greater power. They can now *tell* what happened. Thus Jay, agitated about his brother's having an accident, says to his mother: "He falled on his side and he hurt hisself and he fell down like this." Cathy, accused of putting leaves on her friend Sue, explains: "Sue didn't mind. And Sue did help me pick them up." Mike at 33 months goes over an incident in which something was bought for him and had to be exchanged. "Who bought me this?" Mother: "I did." Mike:

"No, Anna did. And you paid for—um—and down there, and you wait for her. Didn't you? And her change it. And this wasn't right. Other one wasn't right."

Narrative stands out as well in the pleasure with which children plan awful deeds, muttering the story line to themselves in the pleasure of anticipating reactions from others. Jackie, at 36 months, is alone in the garden planning a previously forbidden act: putting sand in a friend's watering can.

13. Family J (Study 2). Child 36 months

C: I'm going to get this in Diana's watering can. Wet cement. When she comes home, she will say "There's sand in the watering can" . . . And she can't water it——put water in it. Sand in it.

M *(enters garden and sees child putting sand in can)*: Look you know what Diana says about that, Jackie. She says that she doesn't like you doing that.

C: I know she doesn't!

And here is Cathy, who after complaining to herself about a scratchy vest that makes her itch, takes it off and hides it with glee:

14. Family R (Study 2). Child 36 months

C: Mummy won't find my vest now (laughs). I put it under— —And now she won't find it!

There is evidently special pleasure, too, in reporting sins committed by themselves. Here is Bill describing his forbidden actions to the observer, with delight:

15. Family T (Study 2). Child 36 months

C: I put my boots on here, and I comed in here, and I put them on again, and I put soil all round the place. In the drawing room. The kitchen. The sitting room. And in the hall!

In the third year these powers of narrative are only just beginning to develop. Children's first steps in telling stories are particularly faltering and confused when they attempt to describe events involving others' actions in the real world that intrigue or puzzle them. In one instance, three-year-old Sammy tries to describe an accident with his father's bicycle: "Daddy— Sally went—And the policeman was there too. In Daddy's spokes. He's got big wheels. Daddy's got big wheels. Daddy can't fall down when he can cycle to college." In another, Zara's account of an incident where a petrol can was thrown into the sea leaves her mother pretty confused: "Grandma made a—I put that thing—I put—we took it to Grandma's and Grandma made it into that thing which she—which she threw in the sea."

In contrast, their own narratives in play, where events are fully under their own control, often go more smoothly and coherently. Most strikingly, telling tall stories of their own devising becomes a pleasure shared by siblings. Danny at 36 months takes delight in a story of multiple Alexanders, with his older brother.

16. Family G (Study 2). Child 36 months

C to sib: Guess what, Tom?

Sib: Yes?

C: Alexander—he met another Alexander. Went to his house and said to Alexander who lives with—who lives over the road—and he said to Alex—um, um—Oh I didn't notice you were Alex. That what he said. Christopher said there was another one. And he looked like Alexander. He was Alexander but he, he, he—guess what Alexander did?

Sib: What?

C: He punched another Alexander. And another Alexander came right, and punched the other one.

Sib: Then another Alexander came along and punched the other one.

C: Yeah. Another one came to punch that one. And another one came and punched that one, and another one came to

punch that one. He's tell me all about that. I saw him.
Fighting with—fighting with the others. Saw him.
Sib: Danny. You just lying.
C: It is! I saw him!

The pleasure of shared deceit and shared jokes is for some siblings a recurring theme in their relationship: what those jokes reveal is the topic we now turn to.

8

Jokes and Humor

Girl (4:9)
(writing letter)
Dear Uncle Poop, I would like you
to give me a roasted meatball, some
chicken pox . . . and some tools.
Signed . . . Mrs. Fingernail. (smiles
and looks up at partner)

Girl (4:7)
(listening)

Toop poop. (laughs) Hey,
are you Mrs. Fingernail?

Yes, I'm Mrs. Fingernail.
(in grand, dignified voice)

Poop, Mrs. Fingernail.
(giggles)
—Children quoted by Catherine Garvey, *Play*, 1977

The development of a child's moral understanding is usually considered in relentlessly serious terms, no matter what century the writer is from. It is the children's sense of guilt, anxiety, fear of adult disapproval, and feeling for the pain of others that are discussed, both by anxious parents of the nineteenth century concerned with their child's conscience and by developmental psychologists of today.

It seems entirely plausible that all these are indeed important in children's growing understanding of what is prohibited, what sanctioned, and of how people in their world respond to cultural breaches. Yet this bleak emphasis on anxiety, guilt, and fear misses one striking feature of young children's social knowledge and of the part that moral issues play in their daily lives. This is that children, even before they are using many words, find the rules, roles, and relationships of their world a source of amusement, of jokes that can be shared with others. Just as children play with a rule of language as soon as they have grasped it, so too they are amused by jokes about what is expected and allowed, what is disapproved of, what is punishable, as soon as they begin to understand those rules. Catherine Garvey comments that "as soon as a child has learned how something is supposed to be, then it becomes a source of fun to distort it or exaggerate it in some way" (1977, p. 70). It is a point that is strikingly true of children's social knowledge, especially for their grasp of the rules of acceptable behavior and of what upsets other people.

Children's sense of what is comic or grotesque in their own or other people's behavior highlights their sense of what is the expected way to behave. To be amused by violation of order or accepted behavior clearly presupposes an understanding of that order. Looking at what children find funny can then give us a window on how they see the people and rules of their world. But it does more than reveal their own categories of usual and unusual behavior. Children's amusement is usually a highly social matter. Sharing a joke implies at some level an expectation that another person will also find this distortion of the expected absurd or comic. It indicates some belief that not only the rule but pleasure in its violation is common to both self and other. There are, of course, jokes that are private to the individual and that carry no implication of shared understanding; these, however, are inaccessible to us as observers. What I will consider here are the exchanges between children and their parents and siblings in which the children laugh or smile, the sources of laughter and glee *between* the children and others in their families. What do children find funny? How does this change as they grow up, and what can it tell us about their social knowledge?

We face the same gap here that was apparent in our inquiries about the development of the child's understanding of others' feelings and intentions and of social rules—a gap between the research on infancy and that on later childhood. There is illuminating work on the smiling and laughter of infants during the first year of life. Alan Sroufe and his colleagues have shown, for instance, how babies tend to be interested in the incongruous:

distortions or exaggerations of familiar events, if not so extreme as to be threatening, make them smile or laugh (Sroufe and Wunsch, 1972). During the first year, children become increasingly able to produce for themselves experiences that amuse them.

For children of three and four years, we have one set of fascinating experiments on the sources of children's laughter, and some amusing studies of children's verbal play. Florence Justin (1932) tested the effectiveness of a number of theories on the causes of laughter, with children of three to six. Was laughter the result of surprise, of violations of expectation, of the perception of incongruity? Was it the result of the release of tension, or of the witnessing of another's misfortune? Was smiling socially elicited, by the observation of someone else's amusement? Her experiments showed that situations designed to test each of these theories all made children smile and laugh. The older children tended to smile for longer and at a wider range of incidents than the younger: with growing understanding, the possibilities of comic distortion clearly increase. But it was evident that already at three years old children were amused by most of the same situations that provoked adult mirth.

For the period between infancy and this preschool stage, we have little systematic information about a child's sense of humor (see Schulz, 1976). Children growing from infancy to childhood are studied remorselessly as creatures who are struggling with emotional problems and "developmental dilemmas" (Heckhausen, 1983), as linguists and as conversationalists, but rarely as humorists. Yet it is clear, from our observations of children in conflict with mothers and siblings, that humor plays a great part in children's daily encounters with their relatives. Breaking the rules of what a parent permits is, as we have seen, a frequent source of amusement to children. In this chapter we look at what makes children laugh and smile not only in conflict situations, but in other exchanges with family members.

It must be noted at the outset that there is a major problem in making inferences about precisely why a child is laughing, in either a naturalistic setting or in an experiment. In Justin's experiments, for instance, it was assumed that if a child laughed when the tester fell off a small chair, the child's laughter resulted from a feeling of superiority at the tester's degradation. The grounds for making the inference seem rather shaky: couldn't the child be responding to the surprise or to the incongruity of the event? The difficulty of deciding what a child is laughing at is particularly acute with observations of very young children who are not using much language. Take some observations of the younger children in our first six-family study:

1. Family N (Study 1). Child 14 months
Mother climbs onto kitchen counter, then onto window sill in order to open jammed window. C watches, points to M, looks at observer and smiles.

2. Family H (Study 1). Child 14 months
Washing machine suddenly makes high squeaky sound. C looks at M and laughs.

3. Family N (Study 1). Child 14 months
M puts rubber gloves on her head and clowns for C. C laughs.

It appears that there is a general class of events here that results in the child's amusement. "Discrepant events," in which people or objects behave in slightly unusual ways, amuse the children, just as they amused the babies in Sroufe and Wunsch's study. Within this broad category there are grouped some very different incidents. In some incidents the person at whom the child laughs is acting intentionally to clown; in other incidents the odd behavior is not apparently done to amuse. It is possible that such distinctions influence the child's response yet it would be fairly hazardous to attempt to interpret what the children find funny. A more cautious approach is to take the crude global grouping of discrepant behavior, recognizing that it probably conflates widely differing incidents.

The other types of event that resulted in smiling or laughing in our observations included five further general categories:

smiles/laughs at forbidden actions; success smiles (seen when the child completed a task or achieved something struggled over); social-facilitation smiles/laughs (when children smiled following the laughter or smiles of another person, without any evidence that they were amused by the actual source of the other person's mirth); smiles/laughs during affectionate play with another, greeting another; smiles/laughs at verbal play or category jokes. For my focus on the development of social knowledge, it is the categories of smiling at discrepant events, at forbidden behavior, at success, and at verbal and category play that are particularly illuminating.

Discrepant events

Discrepant events were already at 14 months a potent source of amusement to the children. Incidents in which children at this age looked at their mother or the observer and smiled or laughed while they themselves or someone else carried out odd actions occurred on average four times an hour. Typical incidents included:

4. Family B (Study 1). Child 14 months
C puts foot in cardboard box and moves it along the floor, with accompanying grating sound. C looks at sibling and laughs.

5. Family D (Study 1). Child 18 months
C puts potty on head, looks at M and observer, and smiles.

Laughing or smiling at such odd behavior continued to occur at roughly the same frequency during the second year. However, the global category of discrepant events masks some interesting developmental changes. In the early months, the events that led to laughter were simple slapstick incidents or incongruities; but the incidents later in the second year included some of considerable elaboration, in which the children themselves played with socially expected behavior. Compare the simple clowning of the girl in example 5 with the behavior of Martin in the next example, also 18 months old but a relatively sophisticated teaser and joker. The focus again is on that significant object, the potty.

> 6. *Family C (Study 1). Child 18 months*
> C sits on potty (fully clothed, not asked to do so), looks at M.

> C: Poo! (grunts heavily). Poo! (grunts). Poo! (gets up, looks at M, picks up empty potty and waves it at M, laughing).

Forbidden actions

While amusement at discrepant events was shown at roughly the same frequency throughout the second year, amusement at forbidden actions increased dramatically over the months, from an average of 1.5 incidents in two hours at 14 months to an average of 6.1 in two hours at 24 months. This amusement was four times more likely to be shown at their own transgressions than at those of other people—but their own transgressions were of course occurring with the highest frequency. Several of the examples given in Chapters 2 and 3 illustrate this amusement at the violation of approved behavior.

Success smiles

A third category of smiling incidents that we examined was that of success smiles, or "mastery smiles" (Kagan, 1981). These are thought to reflect the child's pleasure at achieving a goal; thus increases in the frequency of success smiles are seen as reflecting developments in the child's ability to plan and set goals for himself. In his important study, Kagan reports that mastery smiles were shown with increasing frequency during the second half of the second year, and he links this development to the child's increasing self-awareness (1981, p. 133).

In our Cambridge study, the six children were observed to smile in this way more frequently at 16 than at 14 months, but after that point there was no increase in the frequency of success smiles. What lies behind the difference in the two studies is this: Kagan included in his category of mastery smiles the smiles of a child who "tested the limits" by carrying out a forbidden action, and smiles in this context were shown increasingly frequently over the second year in our study. If we had included these in the category of success smiles, our results would parallel Kagan's. It is important to note here that the influences on the frequency with which children show pleasure at their own mastery are complex and may change during the second year. It is likely, for example, that children during the second year attempt increasingly difficult tasks and are more frequently frustrated—and thus are less often pleased at their own success than the early months of the year. The increase in tantrums over the year supports this view.

Verbal and category jokes

Our study of the six children followed in detail during their second year shows them to be increasingly amused by transgressions of permitted behavior, and effective at teasing in a way that reflects a humorous distortion of usual family interactions. As the children approached 24 months, their amusement was increasingly expressed at verbal jokes, incongruities, and teasing. With the acquisition of linguistic and conversational skills, the possibilities for play with violation of social rules and expectations, conversational conventions, moral issues, truth conditions, and social relations suddenly expand dramatically. Between 18 and 36 months a whole new set of sources of amusement became apparent. The delight of older children in such play with language and social rules has been graphically documented by Catherine Garvey (1977); our two-year-olds are just beginners in this field, but we find many of the same features of humorous play that Garvey describes in four-

and five-year-olds. The examples that follow come from the forty children of Study 2.

Disgust, scatalogical jokes, insults

Play with expressions of disgust and scatalogical jokes were conspicuously common. In the next example the children engage in ritual chanting, of the type described by Garvey in her studies of older children, and two-year-old Laura introduces with delight a variant on the repeated pattern.

7. *Family B (Study 2). Child 24 months*

Sib: Hello, Lollypop Laura!
C: Hello, Lollypop!
Sib: Hello, Lollypop Laura!
C: Hello, Lollypop!
Sib: Hello, Lollypop you!
C: Hello, Lollypop!
Sib: Hello, Lollypop Laura!
C: Hello, Lollypop *Bum*!
Sib: What?

Later in the same observation, the two sisters began a pretend game in which the older is the baby and Laura is the mother.

Sib (lying on her back): Change my bottom, Laura. Change my bottom. Change my bottom.
Child: Yes (pulls her pants off). That's stinky! (laughs).
Sib: You're stinky!
C: Stinky! Stinky! (laughs).
M: Pull her pants up for her, Laura. Laura, pull her pants up. Laura. Pull 'em up. Pull 'em up.
C: Wee wee! Wee wee! (smiles).

These "naughty" words were potent sources of smiles and laughter; the children were tremendously amused when either they themselves or other people used such terms.

8. *Family W (Study 2). Child 36 months*

Sib: (reading paper): Ooh! Smelly!
C (laughs, looks at observer): Ooh! Smelly!

Later in the same observation this boy commented with delighted disgust on his sister's fart:

C: Poo! You shouldn't smell! You shouldn't smell! (laugh).
Sib: (laughs).
C: Poo! Poo!

Great amusement at their own and other's use of forbidden verbal epithets or insults was shown by many of the two- and three-year-olds. In the next example the girl explicitly comments that she isn't allowed to use the term *piggyface,* then does so with glee. Her imitation of her older sister is typical: many of the early examples of such forbidden talk follow directly upon an older sibling's example.

9. *Family B (Study 2). Child 36 months*

Sib: Piggyface!
C: Piggyface!
Sib to observer: I'm not allowed to say Piggyface at school.
C to observer: My mum doesn't let me say Piggyface.
C to sib: Mr. Piggyface! Mr. Piggyface!
Sib: No, not Piggyface.
C: Mr. Piggyface!
Sib: You said Piggyface!
C: Mr. Piggyface!

The ritualistic exchanges of children with their siblings, such as the Lollypop Laura chant and the Piggyface example, were often the framework for an exchange of insults. Surprisingly early, the children were able to take part in ritual exchanges set up by their older siblings and were amused by the jokes made possible by the juxtaposition of inappropriate items in the setting of repetitions.

Mistakes and misnaming

Amusement at the misfortunes and mistakes of other people is of course a major theme in adult humor, and it is already apparent in two-year-olds. The laughter of the child in the next example may have arisen because his mother drew attention to the incongruity of his wearing his sister's pants, but the laugh followed directly on his mother's comment on his father's mistake.

10. Family N (Study 1). Child 21 months

M: Whose trousers have you got on today?
C: Annie's.
M: Mm? Your daddy put you on a pair of Annie's trousers. Silly old Daddy!
C: Yes! (laughs).

Children also show amusement at their own mistakes, and they do of course frequently make mistakes in language and logic, as their older siblings remorselessly point out.

11. Family W (Study 2). Child 36 months
C was corrected, a few minutes earlier, by his sister Ella for referring to his friends as his brothers.

C to observer: My brothers—I mean my—(looks at sibling and both smile). I haven't got some brothers. Ella's my brother.
Sib: (laughs).
C to sib: Are you my brother?
Sib: I'm your sister.
C: Who's my brother then?

The potential importance of such exchanges in the development of social knowledge should not be overlooked.

Naughty and good

Play with what is naughty and what is good, evident in conflict encounters of the second year, continues in the third—but now it is often verbal play on the issue, and play that involves reversal of roles.

12. Family M (Study 3). Child 30 months

C *(boy) to M:* Oh ma Mummy! I smack your bot!
M: Why?
C: You're caughty boy!
M: I'm a girl.
C: No you're caughty boy . . .
Sib: Naughty naughty boy.
C: I not taughty boy. I a girl.
Sib: No, you're not.
C: Yeah.

Jokes about gender and relationships

The child's play on gender in example 12 is echoed in the observations of several other children: such jokes illustrate the confidence with which some children in their third year apply and play with gender. In the next example (Dunn and Kendrick, 1982), the girl plays with the gender identity of herself and her baby brother.

13. Family C (Study 4). Child 32 months

C *(playing with her teddy) to father:* Teddy's a man.
F: What are you?
C: You're a boy.
F: Yeah. What are you?
C: A menace.
F: Yeah, a menace. Apart from that, are you a boy or a girl?
C: Boy (laughs).

F: Are you? What's Trevor?
C: A girl (laughs).
F: You're silly.

The teasing element evident in the last two examples—not giving the expected or accepted answer, not complying or behaving correctly—recurs in a great many of the children's joking encounters with their parents. In the third year, such teasing can take the form of playing both with the emotional dynamics of the relationship and with conversational conventions.

14. Family N (Study 1). Child 24 months

M: Do you like your Mummy, John?
C: No yes! (smiles).
M: No yes? No yes?
C: No yes!

John used the powerful tease of playing on the theme of whether he does or does not like his mother several times during the observations, as did a number of other two-year-old children. The pleasure that such play with the relationship between child and mother generates may well involve what Garvey calls "testing the limits of what another person will tolerate"—a risky business when that other is your mother. Yet taking grave risks appear to be a key feature in the play of adults (Callois, 1961; Goffman, 1971).

In the verbal play of these children with prohibited words, and in their risk-taking teasing of their parents, we see a more elaborate form of the delight in transgression and confrontation evident early in the second year: further evidence for the children's understanding of the rules of their world and of how to upset others. But with the cognitive advances of the second and third year and with the power of language, a new range of resources for humor are available. With language, children play, for instance, with the convention or rule that one should tell the truth. The *joke* of making a false assertion depends, evidently, upon the understanding of this rule, so important in our society. Astonishingly early, the very young boy in the next example makes a category joke by asserting that his milk is beer.

15. Family C (Study 1). Child 21 months
C sitting at table with cup of milk. Looks at observer, points to cup.

C to observer: Beer! (laughs). Beer no!

Jokes about naming are not unusual among two-year-olds: three of the six children followed through the second year made such jokes by the time they were 24 months old. With their limited linguistic skills, these jokes were made simply with negation. One 24-month-old child pointed to a picture of squirrels, looked at the observer, said "Not birds!" and laughed. Another showed a toy toilet seat from her doll's house to the observer and said, smiling, "Not chair!" Even though they were unable themselves to produce inappropriate names or categories of any complexity, they were often much amused by such jokes made by others.

16. Family J (Study 3). Child 28 months
After long exchange in which father asked C what new things he had in his bedroom, and a series of answers was discussed (chair, bed, curtains), sibling made an unexpected contribution.

Sib to child: You had—You had—two fresh pineapples.
C: (laughs).
F to C: Done away with your cot, didn't we? Don't suit the cot anymore, do you?
Sib: You had—you sleep in pineapples instead . . . You don't sleep in your cot. I said you sleep in pineapples.
C (laughing) to M: Sleep in pineapples!

Even earlier, in the second year, some children, in the context of ritualized exchanges with their siblings, enjoyed jokes about incongruous labeling or juxtapositions of unexpected variants on everyday terms. They appeared to appreciate the distortions even though they themselves were not yet able to produce them. In the next example the older sibling takes up a routine care-taking question by the mother and distorts it, to the delight of her young brother:

17. *Family N (Study 1). Child 21 months*

M to C: Do you want a drink?
C: No. Not have drink.
M to C: Well, you don't have to have a drink.
Sib to C: Do you want to drink?
C: No.
Sib to C: Do you want to play?
C: No.
Sib to C: Do you want to coffee?
C: No.
Sib to C: Do you want to eat the windows?
C: Yes! (smiles).
Sib to C: Do you want to eat the heating?
C: Yes! (smiles).
Sib to C: Do you want to eat the windows?
C: Yes!
Sib to C: John, do you want to eat the windows?
C: Yes!

By three years old, children show great delight in inappropriate naming and categorization. In the next example Charlie is delighted by the oddity of the fact that the family cat (Domino) enjoys dog biscuits.

18. *Family P (Study 2). Child 36 months*

Sib to observer: Domino has dog biscuits.
C: Dog biscuits!

Later in the observation Charlie referred back to this oddity by wittily interrupting a conversation between his mother and the observer about food to suggest that we could "try cat biscuits!"

But the enjoyment of deliberate falsehood or misnaming is limited and not very stable to begin with: the two-year-old children's hold on what *is* the case and what *is* the name is not always sufficiently strong for them to enjoy playing with names or with the truth. Anne Davison (1972) studied the beginnings of play with false assertions in two French-speaking siblings. Misnaming things was found funny by the three-year-old, Sophie and also, but less steadily so, by younger brother Jean. He, at 24 months, not only participated in jokes about his own gender (agreeing that he was indeed a girl, in order to be allowed to participate in a game) but on occasion initiated jokes about what was not the case, just as our Cambridge children did. A still younger child in Davison's study, who was at the one-word stage, did not find such "nonserious speech" amusing.

Enjoyment of false assertions sometimes followed serious attempts to understand the real-unreal distinction. Laura in the next example is watching television with her mother and starts a conversation with a serious question about how a dog could be talking.

19. *Family B (Study 2). Child 36 months*
Mother and child watching TV program in which puppet dog and snake are talking.

C: Dogs don't talk.
M: Look, it does talk.
C: They don't.
M: You watch.
C: (laughs).
M: See! The dog talks.
C: Funny dog! Funny dog.
M: He is! There's the snake.
C: Snakes don't talk, do they?

M: Well, that snake's talking now.
C: Not really (laughs). They don't talk really.

The children's confidence in play with false assertions over gender contrasts with their uncertainty, and sometimes unease, over the true/false game when it is played out in other contexts. With this two-year-old, the game was pushed too far.

20. Family N (Study 1). Child 24 months
C, in course of argument with sister, roars with anger.

M: Are you a lion? Is it a lion I've got here?
Sib: yes.
M: Is it? It's making a noise. Is it roaring?
Sib: Yes.
M: I think it's a lion. Is it a roaring lion? Roar then, lion.
C: No. I not a lion. I not a lion. I John (cries).

The same child at 36 months is playing happily with false assertions. In the next example John had begun a fantasy game in which he announced that he was going to burn a neighboring child in a bonfire. When his mother remonstrated, his older sister Annie supported him, giving a false reason for such an action that John delightedly picked up.

21. Same as above. Child 36 months

C: I'm going to burn everyone. I'm going to burn Jimmy I am. To burn Jimmy Green. To burn Jimmy Green . . .
M to C: Well, I think you're horrid. Making fires to burn people.
Sib to M: Anyway he needs to burn Jimmy Green. Because he keeps biting him.
M to sib: He doesn't keep biting him, Annie.
Sib: Yes he does. (To child) Doesn't he, John?
C: Yes he does! He does bite me! You know he does. He does he does he does!

M: I think the boot's on the other foot!
C: No! (laughs).
M: Jimmy Green's a nice quiet little boy.
C: No! (laughs).

The difference between John's delight in maintaining that the "nice quiet little boy" had bitten him (quite untrue) and his upset behavior in example 20 reflects more than an age difference in the confidence with which children play with false assertions. There is an important contrast in the emotional setting of the two exchanges. In the first example, John is initially angry at his sister; when his mother attempts to tease him out of the anger, and she and his sister then unite in discussing whether he is a lion, his fury and distress escalate. His denial may well reflect his fury at his mother and his sister, rather than an age-related inability to cope with a play on false assertions about his own identity. In contrast, the false assertion in example 21 is made by his sister to justify John's action, in the face of his mother's disapproval. It is very much in his own interests to keep this joke going, and he does so with alacrity.

This brings us to an important general point. How children respond to jokes, how and when they themselves joke and the *kind* of joke they make, vary dramatically with particular relationships (with mother, father, or sibling) as well as with the children's current mood and their disposition (cf. Sroufe and Wunsch, 1972, on babies). It was with their siblings that the children enjoyed and developed ritual insults, scatalogical jokes, word play on forbidden topics. With parents, play with naming jokes, true-false assertions, transgression of social rules, and the emotional dynamics of the relationship stand out. In such differences we see again the sensitivity of these very young children to the differences in their family relationships. They already have considerable grasp of what familiar others will find funny or offensive; they understand which rules can be played with and with whom.

Furthermore, the quality of humor and amusement that the child and partner enjoy in a particular relationship is no trivial feature of that relationship—a point we would surely concede in terms of our own relationships, yet one that is almost entirely neglected by child psychologists. What features of the mother child relationship are studied? The child's sense of security or insecurity in the attachment, the mother's sensitivity, responsiveness, warmth, or controlling behavior—but rarely their joking or sense of fun, their rapport over the absurdities of everyday life. Yet that rapport and shared amusement can, we all know, transform the most mundane daily routines into happy and exciting events. It is surely not a minor or unimportant developmental achievement that children already in their second and third year are able to join successfully in the very different jokes of their parents and their siblings, and are able to make those people laugh.

Laughing and learning?

Looking at what makes children smile and laugh shows that children as they move from infancy to childhood are increasingly amused by violation of rules, by what causes disgust or disapproval to others. As two-year-olds they explore and exploit the possible distortions of what is accepted in different ways with their siblings and with their mothers, managing to share different jokes with two very different family members. Between 24 and 36 months they take part, with pleasure, in jokes about *relationships* (I don't love you, Mummy!), about gender, about what is naughty or disgusting, about truth and falsehood, about others' mistakes, and about incongruities in family routines. From these observations we gain another view of their developing social understanding, and some sense of a central dimension of their relationships that as psychologists we have ignored too long. But is it possible that in such joking exchanges children's social understanding is not only revealed but fostered? Are children learning in the course of such interactions?

I have already commented on the difficulty of establishing precisely when children make developmental advances. With naturalistic observations we can only speculate, never establish with certainty the developmental significance of particular interactions. But a number of features of these joking interactions stand out as potentially important in children's learning. By definition these joking exchanges are playful—and it has been argued that the very nature of playful exchanges makes them important as contexts in which children are likely to learn. Clearly it is inappropriate to look for a single function in play. Play at different stages of development, and with different resources, presumably has different functions. Yet it has been argued convincingly by Susannah Millar (1968) that the usefulness of play activities is related to their occurrence at the early stages of the development of particular competencies. Bruner, in discussing the significance of playful exchanges between child and mother for language acquisition, cites a number of features of playful interaction as important for the development of language (for example, Bruner and Sherwood, 1976). Of these, three are also relevant to the potential of the joking exchanges I have described for social learning. First, in playful exchanges the structure of the routine and the semantic domain are highly restricted and well understood by the child, but amenable to having their constituents varied; second, the role structure is reversible; third, the playful atmosphere of the interactions permits the child to distance himself in a way that sustains his readiness to innovate.

The emotional atmosphere of many of the interactions observed was undoubtedly one in which the children could happily try things out. And in some cases it was clear that important social categories were in fact being clarified for the children—for instance, the categories of real-unreal (example 19), of friend-brother-sister (example 11), of gender (examples 12, 13). The suggestion is not that playful conversations are the only contexts in which a child's confusion over such categories is clarified. But they are likely to be one of the more important ones, as Tizard and Hughes (1984) have argued from their evidence from the conversations between four-year-olds and their mothers.

Less obvious but developmentally important is the potential of the teasing exchanges with parent or sibling for learning the limits of acceptability of insult, criticism, or expression of dislike within an important emotional relationship. Most difficult of all to establish—but in commonsense terms perhaps the most plausible—is the importance of the experience of shared jokes and amusement in the developing relationship between child and mother, child and sibling. Discovering how to share a sense of absurdity and pleasure in the comic incidents of life is an important step toward intimacy.

9

Implications

What is the nature of young children's understanding of other people and of their social world as they grow from infancy to childhood? How does this understanding change and what influences its development? With these ambitious questions in mind, we have looked at children's behavior in conflict, in play, in conversation with their mothers and siblings. The evidence leads to an argument—set out initially in Chapter 4 on the basis of the analysis of the children's behavior in conflict—with two components. The first concerns children's practical understanding of their family world; the second, the connections between the development of this understanding and children's emotional relationships, their developing sense of self and self-concern, and the moral discourse of that world.

The nature of young children's understanding

In theories of moral development concerned with the ability of individuals to articulate judgments in relation to hypothetical dilemmas (Kohlberg, 1976), our two- and three-year-olds would have no place. Yet the evidence from the observations shows that children from 18 months on understand how to hurt, comfort, or exacerbate another's pain; they understand the consequences of their hurtful actions for others and something of what is allowed or disapproved behavior in their family world; they anticipate the response of adults to their own and to others' misdeeds; they differentiate between transgressions of various kinds. They comment and ask about the causes of others' actions and feelings. Four features of this understanding stand out for emphasis.

Understanding others' feelings. Children's understanding

grows early in the second year from an "affective tuning" to the distress and amusement of others—beginning with the "affective resonance" of the first year described by Stern (1985)—to a grasp of how certain actions lead to the anger and disapproval of others, of what transgressions can be a shared source of amusement with others, and of what actions can comfort a mother's or a sibling's distress. Children respond empathetically to the distress of others early in the second year, and more generally they are *interested* in the feeling states of others; they show, both in their nonverbal behavior and increasingly explicitly in their verbal behavior during the third year, attention to, curiosity about, and understanding of the causes of pain, distress, anger, pleasure and displeasure, comfort, and fear in others as well as themselves. They joke, play with, and tell stories about these feeling states in self and other. Their responsivity to the feeling states of others (Blum, 1987) shows us that the foundations for the moral virtues of caring, considerateness, and kindness are well laid by three years.

Understanding others' goals. Children in their second year develop increasing sensitivity to the goals and intentions of others, a sensitivity that is evident in their behavior in conflict, in their helpful and cooperative behavior, and in the third year in their pretend games, narratives, and questions about others.

Understanding social rules. From this sensitivity to the emotions and goals of other family members grows an interest in transgressions of acceptable or expected behavior and an understanding of social rules and family relationships. Children differentiate between certain kinds of transgression, in their emotional behavior and in their attempts to reason. They question and discuss the differential application of rules to different people and joke with others about transgressions.

This understanding of others' feelings and the use of social rules become rapidly more elaborated and more explicitly articulated during the third year. We don't yet have grounds for referring to "structural" changes or "stages" in these aspects of understanding (in contrast, perhaps, with the evidence on children's understanding of mind). But our observations show that by two and a half to three years of age, children demonstrate a practical knowledge of the idea of responsibility, of excuses of intent and incapacity, of how rules apply differently to different family members and how they can be questioned, of how transgressions can be justified. They have begun to understand something of the authority relations within the family and to comment on the behavior of others in moral terms. Moral understanding depends in part upon a child's general knowledge about the social world; what our observations show is that children even in their second and third years have a far subtler comprehension of their social world than we have given them credit for. They are faced, even as two- and three-year-olds, with issues of caring, support for and alliance with those in distress or conflict—issues that are increasingly stressed in discussions of moral development (for instance, Gilligan, 1982)— and they have a ready-to-hand way of dealing with them (Packer, 1985).

The argument that these very young children have an implicit grasp of the distress that another feels when hurtful acts are inflicted, of the response of parental disapproval to forbidden acts, and of the amusement that a sibling will feel at certain transgressions does not imply that they have explicit or detailed social knowledge. Rather, it parallels Gelman's and Baillargeon's argument (1983) concerning the conceptual development of preoperational children: that such children have some implicit knowledge of counting, conservation, and arithmetical principles well before they have explicit understanding of the principles. As noted in Chapter 1, the demonstration of both explicit and implicit knowledge depends crucially upon the nature of the setting and the task. With development, children's understanding becomes increasingly explicit, and they are able to make use of their capabilities in an inceasingly wide range of situations. What the observations reported here show is that in the familiar and emotional exchanges between family members, especially those in which their own interests are at stake, children have a practical grasp of some of the causes of states of distress, anger, and happiness in other family members, and of certain rules and roles in that family world, from early in their second year. We cannot of course assume that they would show such understanding of unfamiliar others or of social rules in an unfamiliar setting or in situations that do not engage their self-interest.

What should not pass unnoticed is the nature of the rules they articulate and use. The bases for their excuses, justifications, and jokes include not only the idiosyncratic practices of a particular family, but some of the key principles of the wider culture outside the family: principles of possession, positive justice, excuses on grounds of incapacity or lack of intention, even gender-role division of labor. The context specificity of the child's grasp of these principles remains an important but unexplored issue. From the basis of our observations, we can say that some of these principles are understood not in a highly context-specific way but much more broadly. The three-year-old's sense of possession rights or of the significance of sharing is certainly not limited to himself and his immediate family or peers. To argue that *ladies* use vacuum cleaners is to make a general, normative claim.

On the other hand, there is also evidence that children of this age can learn extremely fast about certain context-specific rules and do not make mistakes about applying them in other contexts. Thus a study by Carol Kendrick (1986) shows that children (even those as young as three) who were in the hospital suffering from leukemia grasped features of ward life very fast indeed—and explained these features to their parents. They understood, for example, that you could talk to a nurse in a certain way that you could not talk to a doctor, that certain medical procedures happened whether you fussed or not but that others could be battled over. Nancy Much and Richard Shweder (1978) in their studies of children in nursery school show similarly that children have a clear grasp of context-specific (in this case, school-specific) rules. And what is striking about the children's grasp of more general rules, such as gender-appropriate behavior, is their growing sensitivity to how such rules can be used differentially within different relationships. Shirley Brice-Heath makes the same point vividly in her observations of the two-year-olds on the porches and streets of the community she studied in North Carolina. The main task facing the children was how to differentiate when and where to employ particular strategies and rules, in a world in which adults and older children behave in a notably varied and inconsistent way.

The findings from the hospital study poignantly highlight one implication of the observations discussed in this book: children can learn very fast about rules when the context is emotionally urgent. A provocative parallel here is the work of Leda Cosmides, showing how much better adults manage on tasks that have content of social significance than they do on tasks with the same logical problems but more abstract content, findings she incorporates into a general argument that the human mind evolved to solve social, domain-specific problems—an evolutionary argument with which the evidence considered in this book certainly does not conflict (Cosmides, 1985; Cosmides and Tooby 1987).

Understanding other minds? In the course of the third year, children begin to talk about knowing, remembering, forgetting—about mental states in themselves and in others (Shatz, Wellman, and Silber, 1983; Wellman, 1986). Wellman argues plausibly on the basis of experimental and naturalistic studies that, between two and a half and three years, children have an understanding of mind that is a coherent and interconnected body of concepts, that makes a clear distinction between mental and physical entities. The observations of our Cambridge studies show that, along with this evidence for the beginnings of the ability to reflect on other minds, there is a growth of disinterested curiosity about the social world, a new curiosity about others, evident in children's questions and narratives. It appears that, as children's ideas about others and the social world become clearer, their theories about other people become more elaborate, and it follows that there are more issues to clarify with questions. These developments in the ability to conceive of other minds in the second half of the third year have such profound consequences for children's understanding of their social world and their communication that a reasonable case can be made for designating this a new "stage" in children's social understanding.

The discrepancy between these powers of understanding and those that would be attributed to the children on the basis of their response to hypothetical storybook situations parallels the discrepancy noted by Spelke and Cortelyou (1981) in the perceptual abilities of babies when these are assessed in different ways:

> Studies of perception of face photographs and drawings suggest a slow development of sensitivity to other people (cf. Carey and Diamond, 1977). Studies of social interaction suggest a rather remarkable competence to perceive others and to participate in social exchanges early in life.
>
> In which view may we trust? Are students of face perception missing the infant's greatest capacities by focussing on impoverished stimulus displays? Or are students of social interaction inflating their estimates of the infant's abilities by focussing on situations in which the infant has an enormous prop: an adult partner who can regulate the social exchange? (p. 80).

In the family confrontations, conversation, and play we have studied, children are indeed interacting with others who are more able to articulate and manipulate the social situation, and they are surely learning from them. Yet the child's capability cannot be simply attributed to the prop of a more sophisticated partner. Unlike the infants in the studies of face perception, observed in playful interaction with adults, the children we have studied often had goals and intentions at odds with those of other people. Indeed this difference in the goals can be, I have argued, of real importance in contributing to a child's learning about others. The observations show us, then, that the tentative suggestions made by Gelman and Spelke (1981) and by Hoffman (1981), with which I began in Chapter 1, are well founded and can be asserted with confidence. Children in their second and third year do indeed have a growing grasp of the permissibility of actions and of the feelings of others; they also have a burgeoning curiosity about the social world.

It is of course the very beginnings of understanding the social world that we see in these young children. The limitations of their understanding are obvious. We have, for instance, no evidence for any ability to recognize the subtler shades of emotional states, of embarrassment, shame or guilt, or despondency. And experimental studies indicate that comprehension of *combinations* of emotions is far off. Clearly the children's grasp of the causes of many adult emotions is likely to be rudimentary, just as their grasp of others' intentions and goals is likely to be limited to the goals of familiar others in familiar contexts—especially those involving the children themselves. Their inability to grasp the intentions of others is poignantly evident in incidents where their older siblings deceive them.

Similarly, their understanding of social rules is limited to those rules that impinge closely upon their own experiences or interests. And passages of "intellectual search," in which they persistently attempt to clarify issues they don't comprehend, are still rare. Finally, their "theory of mind" is importantly limited. Although they understand that mental entities are different from physical ones, and that human action is governed by wishes, beliefs, and attitudes, they do not have a concept of mind as an interpreting, mediating processor of information (Johnson and Wellman, 1982; Wellman, 1986). They have made a critical first step toward understanding this sense of mind, but it is still only a first step.

The development of understanding

Whether we choose to label the understanding these children demonstrate as *moral* or as *social* understanding, its development deserves our attention. My concern in this book has not been to demonstrate that children show certain capabilities several months—or years—earlier than previously suspected, but rather to explore the questions of why and how such abilities develop and are demonstrated. What the observations and argument presented here indicate is that there are striking features of this development neglected by current theories of moral and sociocognitive development. I take it as a given that cognitive changes are involved in the dramatic developments in a child's ability to reflect on others and the social world. But the growth of this understanding involves more than an unfolding of cognitive abilities. Our observations suggest that the following features may also be central.

Self-concern and self in a social world. The drive to understand others and the social world is closely linked to the nature of the child's relationships within the family over this period: the emotional power of attachment to parents, of the conflict between growing independence and socialization, of rivalry with siblings. The urgency of self-assertion in the face of powerful others increases along with the child's understanding. Driving self-concern characterizes much of children's behavior toward other family members in this age period as they develop a new sense of themselves and an increased capacity to plan and achieve goals; and this self-interest invests the understanding of others and of rules with particular salience. Analysis of conversational interventions shows us how strongly the interest in self continues in the third year, notwithstanding children's burgeoning interest in others at this time.

The term *self-interest* has a pejorative tone. But my argument is that we should think of the child's self-concern in a different way. Let us consider, for instance, its relation to the child's developing sense of self. Much of the consideration of self-awareness in the second year has, as we saw in Chapter 4, focused upon the self as "an active cognitive construction" (Harter, 1983). But think for a moment about the child's developing sense of self in terms of her sense of efficacy and control. As Susan Harter points out, this is a critical dimension of self-evaluation. She quotes Cooley, writing in 1902, for whom self-feeling

> appears to be associated chiefly with ideas of the exercise of
> power, of being a cause ... The first definite thoughts that a

child associates with self-feeling are probably those of his earliest endeavours to control visible objects—his limbs, his playthings, his bottle, and the like. Then he attempts to control the actions of the persons about him, and so his circle of power and self-feeling widens without interruption to the most complex of mature ambition. (pp. 145–146)

More recent writers also emphasize the sense of cause as a crucial feature of the sense of self. Thus Bannister and Agnew (1977) comment: "We entertain a notion of ourselves as causes, we have purposes, we intend, we accept a partial responsibility for the effects of what we do. This construing of ourselves as agent is clearly a superordinate contribution toward a total construction of a self" (p. 102).

Now the problems that young children face in social relationships are considerable: how to get others' attention and cooperation, how to cope with disagreements, how to understand another's intentions, how to provide comfort for another who is in distress—how to manage their social world. A child's sense of self-efficacy is likely to come, then, in large part from solving these problems, from having control over such social matters. In being effective in these matters, a core of children's feelings about themselves is established. The significance of this point is brought home to us, powerfully, by the current work on the connections between attributional style and depression in childhood (Seligman and Peterson, 1986).

The achievement of a sense of self-efficacy from managing such aspects of social relationships clearly should not be equated with the satisfaction of self-interest at the expense of the interests of others. Indeed, it is important to note that it does not necessarily imply opposition to the interests of others. Rather, recall Blum's notion of self that has built into it a sense of relatedness to others, and his argument that concern for others—in friendship, for example—is not separable from concern for self. There are two points here. First, a broad concern with self does not *necessarily* imply opposition to the interests of others. In the context of disputes, yes. But part of being effective within the social world is finding ways to help and cooperate with others and also to achieve the approval of others. Second, to be effective entails monitoring the response of others to oneself, their approval or disapproval, pleasure or displeasure. And, as we have seen, children's interest in the realm of what is approved and disapproved by others is wide and persistent by their third year, evident in their narratives, jokes, and questions.

What this suggests is that, although it is generally assumed that children cannot stand back as observers of self until middle childhood, cannot see themselves as others see them, their evident interest in others' affective reactions to their behavior and their responsiveness to approval or disapproval indicates that a new curiosity about how others think about the child grows during the second and third year. Two sets of evidence can help to clarify the question of when children begin to monitor others' reactions to them. First, there is the issue of when children begin to show shame and guilt. It seems that it is during the third year (Barrett, 1987), at least in the presence of others. Although experimental studies suggest that children do not reflect on self-as-others-see-me when directly questioned (Harter, 1983), if they do indeed show shame, embarrassment, and guilt they must at some level be monitoring the response of others to their actions. They certainly make self-evaluative comments in the course of daily family life.

Second, young children do show an interest in comparing themselves to others (Dinner, 1976; Masters, 1971; Ruble, Feldman, and Boggiano, 1976), especially within the family (Dunn and Kendrick, 1982), even though studies that examine children's use of self-comparison in experimental problem solving find that self-comparison in these contexts is not used until middle childhood, around the age of eight (Ruble et al., 1980). The discrepancy between these findings is instructive. It seems that the motivation for making comparisons between self and others is different in different social situations, and that there are developmental changes in children's interest in making social comparisons within these different contexts. A key observation for my focus on the links between self and self-interest is this: The earliest interest in social comparison is concerned with "making sure one is getting one's fair share and is being treated like the other children" (Harter, 1983, p. 358). That is, a concern for the child's own interests pushes the child to make social comparisons, and the processes that begin there are later important in self-evaluation in terms of the social group.

Thus a sense of efficacy in matters of social relationships is an important feature of developing self-awareness. Children begin to make social comparisons in the context of self-interest. The earliest stages of self-awareness are, that is, linked to children's concern over their own interests and their pleasure in social efficacy. There is, moreover, in our daily life a continuing discussion and attribution of blame and responsibility, and frequent comparative comments about family members—conversations in which evaluative judgments about people are both implicitly and explicitly made. Children monitor and join in these conversations from an early age, as our observations have shown and as the following example from Study 4 illustrates. Andy, aged 30 months, has an ebullient, assertive younger sister Susie, aged 14 months; he himself is a notably cautious, anxious, and sensitive child, described by his mother as frightened of his younger sister. He overhears his mother's proud comment on his sister and adds a muted—but accurate—comment on himself in comparison:

M to sib: Susie, you *are* a determined little devil!
C to M: I'm not a determined little devil.
M (laughing): No you're not! What are you? A poor old boy!

In short, children's curiosity about others' behavior, their interest in approval, disapproval, compliance, and transgression, and their continuing concern with self, together with the frequent attributions, evaluations, and comparisons of family discourse, combine to set the stage for the development of a sense of how others evaluate them. How culturally specific such patterns are remains to be explored.

Pleasure from social effectiveness. Children's pleasure in becoming effective family members is evident not only in incidents of conflict but in their negotiation and organization of play, in their interventions in conversation (deflecting the conversations to themselves), in their ability to help others effectively, and to make and share jokes. Mastery of the social world is not only a matter of winning arguments—yet a child's delight in becoming an effective participant in friendly and joking family exchanges in no way conflicts with the proposal that self-concern is a powerful motivating force in the growth of social understanding.

The importance of affective experience. Emotion plays a considerable part in the interactions in which moral and social rules are articulated. The feeling expressed by parent, by sibling, or by child is often highly marked, and the children we studied were in their third year more likely to reason in those disputes that had earlier caused them most distress and anger. They also showed much delight and amusement over transgressions. Distress, anger, and amusement highlight the salience of disputes, frustration of goals, and transgression of rules for the children; these emotions may contribute to the learning that takes place during such interactions. Two points should be emphasized. First, to stress the potential of such affectively loaded interactions for learning is not to argue that understanding others is fostered solely within contexts of heightened emotion. It is clear that children's passages of intellectual search into the social world often take place in conversations with mothers when the child is calm and reflective (see also Tizard and Hughes, 1985). Humans are adaptable creatures who are likely to learn about the world in a variety of settings. My point is that it is not only in calm and reflective situations that children will learn. Rather there may be special potential in the emotionally urgent situations that occur within the family. These are the situations that psychologists have—inevitably—rarely studied; their accounts of cognitive development reflect the contexts in which they have chosen to study children.

Second, the emphasis on emotion in this account differs from other models of early moral development, for example those of

Hoffman (1983) and Kagan (1984). In my view it is the nature of the child's close relationships, rather than socialization pressure, guilt, anxiety, or fear, that is important in these early years: the affective tension in the relationships between siblings and between child and parent provides one important impetus for the child to understand others and the social world. The motivation to understand the world, according to this view, is linked to the child's part in the power relations of the family, not solely, or even primarily, to a wish to allay guilt or to conform.

In contrast, the accounts of Hoffman and Kagan each emphasize the guilt and fear experienced by children when they fail to live up to the standards set by their parents. Hoffman proposes that initially children feel empathy toward distressed others (empathy that is not necessarily mediated by complex cognitive processes) and that during the second year, with the development of a sense of self, children come to distinguish between their own and others' distress. Their understanding of what is moral behavior comes primarily from parental socialization techniques, and the internalization of these norms of prosocial behavior leads children to experience their "moral" behavior as self-produced. The disciplinary encounters between parent and child are crucial in this process, and the child's emotions of guilt, fear, or anxiety during such encounters are seen as central in motivating subsequent moral behavior.

Thus both Hoffman and Kagan link the development of empathy in very young children, the developing concept of self, and the emotions of anxiety, guilt, and fear experienced when children fail to live up to the standards of socialization set by their parents. The emphasis on the connections between emotion, self-awareness, and standards is illuminating and important. Yet my findings suggest a rather different framework for understanding the development of moral understanding. In contrast to the emphasis on guilt and fear, I would argue that a wide range of affective experiences with others is significant. The importance of the positive experiences within the mother-child relationship has been noted in other discussions of

Hoffman's model (for instance Maccoby and Martin, 1983; Rest, 1983). What my observations add to such criticisms is the demonstration of the pleasure and excitement that children experience in *transgressing* rules, in *confronting* and *teasing*— that is, in exerting power within their family world as well as in happy cooperative play and shared amusement.

This emphasis on the child's active enjoyment of such exchanges illustrates how the child's role as an active participant in social interaction, which is indeed stressed by Hoffman, is given a different focus here. The observations draw our attention to the way that children use their growing social understanding within the politics of the family. The children's role is emphasized not simply as a factor that influences the nature of parental socialization practices and expectations; instead children are seen as active agents developing their understanding of the social world partly for their own self-concern. Thus the child's growing cognitive and communicative skills not only influence the parents' strategies in disciplinary encounters; they affect the child's ability to develop plans and put them into practice, to precipitate discussion of rules and relationships, to participate in role-taking games, and to marshal arguments, excuses, and justifications.

A note on cultural differences: The argument presented here has emphasized the significance of the emotions experienced and expressed by children in moments of frustration and confrontation and in shared amusement and pleasure. It is possible that such emotion is *itself* deeply influenced by the culture. We know that there are radical differences between cultures—even within the United States—in such expressions of emotion. Peggy Miller's work with black working-class families in Baltimore has vividly shown that social and moral standards are critically implicated in the socialization of anger and aggression and that these differ with different cultural groups (Miller and Sperry, 1987). These standards are conveyed by the mother's differential response to children's anger in different contexts, by the mother's implicit socialization practices—notably her narratives and by her own demonstrations of anger toward others.

The evidence for children's sensitivity to others suggests that children learn especially fast about such issues and will learn to use emotions instrumentally. But we are still unable to trace cultural differences in developmental patterns with any specificity. It could be that the socialization of emotions takes place chiefly with children older than three, and that the frustration of goals and the sharing of amusement are features of the lives of young children common to most cultures. The examples of incidents leading to anger and distress in the Kipsigis children of Kokwet (Harkness and Super, 1985) are remarkably similar to our observations of Cambridge children. Yet it is also likely that the central significance of possession for western children in family disputes would not be found in less affluent cultures. At any rate, it is clear that not only the emotional experiences but the discourse in family interchanges are of major significance.

Contribution of social discourse. From their first year, children are active participants in discourse about the social rules of their world. It is through the implicit and explicit messages in this moral discourse that they learn much of the nature of the rules of their particular culture. Differences in how these rules are articulated are systematically related to later differences in the children's moral behavior. The socialization experiences within disciplinary encounters that Hoffman stresses are not the only situations in which moral messages are conveyed. The argument advanced here is that many other exchanges may also contribute to the child's growing understanding of the moral order of his world. Children receive messages at every moment of their day about the proper way to live, and they witness such messages sent to others. Disciplinary encounters represent one important context in which such messages are given and received, but it is only one context among many. Messages are clearly not limited to punitive or prohibiting encounters. The child's motivation to behave in a way that is acceptable to his or her parents may be heavily influenced by parental disciplinary strategies. But the development of the child's *understanding* of what is acceptable is influenced by a far wider range of experiences.

The comparison of interactions with parents and with siblings is useful here. Some features of a child's moral behavior—cooperative behavior, conciliatory behavior with siblings—are rarely articulated or taught by adults; instead they are apparently fostered by particular relationships, especially those with other children. We noted that specific encouragement or instruction for cooperation between siblings was rarely given in conflicts between parents and children. Encouragement for the development of cooperation in play depends, it seems, on other social influences: the excitement and pleasure generated in joint games, the motivation to reach a goal shared with another, appear to be likely candidates. Similarly, the development of an early ability to explore social roles and rules within a pretend framework is fostered by an affectionate relationship with a sibling rather than with a mother.

This distinction between what is learned in interaction with adults and what is learned with other children is a central theme in Piaget's account of the development of moral understanding. Disciplinary encounters between child and parent were seen by Piaget in his influential book *The Moral Judgment of the Child* (1932) as initially important in influencing very young children to act in prescribed and morally acceptable ways. But a central theme in his argument was that this "morality of constraint"— a morality of duty and heteronomy based on respect and fear of powerful adults—was very limited. He thought that there was a fundamental change in the nature of children's morality as they grew up and better understood the nature of the social world, in particular as they grasped the importance of cooperation for mutual benefit. A "morality of cooperation" develops, Piaget argued, as with cognitive development children begin to understand that cooperation can lead to mutually useful goals and that social rules can be applied to coordinate such actions.

The contrasts between these two moralities were many, in Piaget's account; their origins, dynamics, and significance for later moral behavior all differed. In particular he contrasted the roles of adults and peers. Because of the equal power relations between peers, children interacting with other children learn about cooperation and the concept of justice as they reason, persuade, and negotiate in joint activities. With the difference in status and power between children and adults, such developments were unlikely to take place in the context of parent-child relationships. Piaget's discussion of morality focuses primarily on the concept of justice, in which society's rules balance the costs and benefits among members of society in a fair way. The morality of constraint—blind obedience to adult rules—does not, he suggested, provide a basis for any deep understanding of the idea of mutual benefit or the concept of justice.

Yet it is clear from the results described here that a sharp contrast between the potential developmental significance of children's disputes with their mothers and with their older siblings is not justified. Cooperation and argument take place with both mother and sibling; the children's growing grasp of principles of positive justice and their notions of rights are evident in their interaction with all family members. Moreover, the processes by which these ideas take hold begin very early, in the context of family life: they do not depend for their genesis upon the arguments of six-year-old children with peers about the rules of games. Watching children at home shows us that it is a matter of urgency and developmental importance for young children to grasp such ideas in their daily family life from early in the second year.

And it is a *family* world of discourse about moral and social matters in which children grow up. Parents and siblings talk to them about the social world from their infancy; they also talk to each other about such matters, and young children, as we have seen, monitor and often comment on these interactions. Their active role in family discourse is evident from the early months of the second year, when they draw attention to transgressions, precipitate discussion of their own and others' behavior, and make jokes about such issues. Social understanding is an instrument in their relationships, and as such it grows, differentiates, and becomes increasingly subtle. Here, then, is the core of the difference between my account—a model of the development of social understanding that emphasizes the nature and role of the child's family relationships—and Piaget's. Piaget is surely right to emphasize that the important developmental exchanges are not those in which social influence is impressed upon children, but those in which they attempt to argue, justify, and negotiate. But my account stresses the significance of the affective dynamics of the relationships that motivate the child to engage in discourse about the social world, rather than solely the cognitive conflict of being faced with another person's point of view. It is the motivation to express himself within the relationship, to cooperate, to get his way or to share amusement, that, I suggest, in part leads the child to discover the ways of the family world.

A "relationships" model of the development of social understanding

All these features suggest a model of the growth of social understanding in which development starts from the child's interest in and responsiveness to the behavior and feelings of others. In the subsequent development of social understanding, contributions are made, first, by the intensity of the child's self-concern in the context of family relationships and, second, by the child's participation in the moral discourse of the family. In other words, the model gives weight both to the cognitive changes that lead to the child's developing sense of self and ability to participate in argument, and to the affective significance of the tension between this self-concern and the child's relationships with other family members. In discourse about the social world, both the affective and the cognitive messages are significant.

The observations and the model raise more questions than they answer. We need to specify further the nature of these interconnections among the increasing cognitive capabilities of the child, the affective relationships of the family world in which those abilities develop, the moral discourse of the family, and the child's affective experiences. We need to clarify the quality and limitations of the capabilities of children over the second and third years. We need to examine the question of whether affective experiences are of special importance in the second as opposed to the third and fourth years—whether, with the development of increased communicative skills, affective experiences become less important in increasing understanding. We need, it is clear, research strategies that use a variety of approaches, experimental as well as naturalistic. Experimental studies such as those demonstrating children's sensitivity to the social situation (Cummings, Zahn-Waxler, and Radke-Yarrow, 1981; Feiring, Lewis, and Starr, 1984), their ability to learn from observing interaction between others, and the significance of verbal explanations accompanying others' actions for children as young as 18 months (Hay et al., 1985) extend what we can learn from naturalistic studies. The argument presented here is in part about what motivates children to understand their world, about what can elicit developmental change; yet naturalistic observations cannot in themselves establish cause, any more than experimental studies can show what contributes to development in the real world.

We need studies that will clarify the causes of the individual differences in children—strikingly apparent in every aspect of behavior discussed. There is no necessary connection between the processes that influence the general "normative" developments explored here and those that influence the development of individual differences. To argue that the normative growth of self-concern in the second year is linked to children's interest in understanding others does not imply that those children whose self-interest is most frequently threatened will show the most advanced social reasoning. But some of the processes we have considered *may* be important in contributing to individual differences. Differences in emotional experiences, in the discourse of the family, and in the qualities of the relationships with sibling and mother are plausible candidates as influences on the development of individual differences in social understanding. Indeed, our findings on the correlations between family discourse about feelings, needs, and intentions and later differences in the children, and on the correlations between children's experiences with their siblings in joint pretend play and the children's later sociocognitive capabilities, support such an argument.

We need, too, studies that focus on cultures that differ from our own in what is approved social practice. We have looked at children growing up within and learning about only one culture, with—inevitably—a particular set of moral and social rules. But the interest of children in their social world and their propensity to use an understanding of that world in their important relationships is surely not particular to one culture. Mongolian children understand by their second year that they must sit only in certain sections of the family tent; children in the Solomon Islands learn that sibling caregivers can be disobeyed and exploited in some circumstances but not in others; children in Cambridge know that swear words can be used to tease adults and to amuse older siblings. The particulars vary, but what is common to all children growing up in families is the importance of understanding what is allowed or disapproved and how others will respond to their behavior. Theories that focus on details of moral reasoning predict cultural differences; the argument presented here predicts common features in children's developing understanding across cultures, given the similarity in children's emotional interests in families everywhere. We would expect differences in children's behavior related to the differences in verbal articulation of rules, differences in the particular rules in question, differences in the individuals as outcomes— but commonalities in the concern of children for the feelings, goals, and behavior of those who share their family world.

Our observations reveal a growing participation in the cultural and emotional world of the family and, as a consequence, in the wider social world beyond. Consider the argument that Jerome Bruner has put forward concerning the cultural understanding revealed by a child's use of language over these months. What he suggests is that children's understanding of the culturally appropriate use of requests, invitations, and reference develops well before they are correctly using conventional linguistic forms. Moreover, "Learning to request is not just learning language or even just speech acts. It is learning the culture and how to get things done in that culture." Similarly Bruner argues that the achievement of reference by the child depends on mastery of social procedures, and he emphasizes the role of mothers in teaching the cultural constraints surrounding the use of such forms:

> In a variety of ways, then—and some are quite subtle—these mothers teach their children just as they are on the brink of lexico-grammatical speech that requests *ask* not *compel,* that they are made only for services that one cannot do oneself, and that they must not demand "excessive" effort from another . . . The "lessons" are obviously as much cultural as they are linguistic. (1983, p. 103)

Bruner's proposal is that language acquisition is a by-product and a vehicle of cultural transmission; the motivation to use language is "the need to get on with the demands of the culture." It is an argument clearly paralleled by the observations and inferences that I have described here. The mastery of cultural matters takes place during those months of the second and third year in which we have seen the children's growing grasp of what is acceptable and unacceptable behavior, and of the power politics within the family. The argument that children begin to use language not because they have a language-using device but because they need to get things done in the culture is echoed, but given a different emphasis. My proposal is that children are motivated to understand the social rules and relationships of their cultural world *because they need to get things done in their family relationships.* What we see in the disputes, jokes, and cooperative actions of the second and third years, and the delight in narrative and pretend play, is the child's increasing subtlety as a member of a cultural world—a subtlety achieved in part because of the pressure of the individual's needs and relationships within that world.

Appendix 1

Participants and Methods

The families taking part in the Cambridge studies were recruited through advertisement in a local newspaper and through the help of Health Visitors. In Study 1, six families took part when the second-born child was aged 14, 16, 18, 21, and 24 months old. There were two sister pairs, two younger sister–older brother pairs, and two younger brother–older sister pairs. In Study 2, forty-three families took part when the secondborn child was 18, 24, and 36 months old. There were nine sister pairs, eight brother pairs, thirteen younger sister–older brother pairs, and thirteen younger brother–older sister pairs. In Study 3, six families took part when the secondborn child was 24, 26, 28, 30, 33, and 36 months old; there were three sister pairs, one brother pair, one younger sister–older brother pair, and one younger brother–older sister pair.

The families were, in terms of the father's occupation, largely middle-class and upper working-class. The occupation of the father classified according to the Registrar General (1973) was I/II (professional and managerial) for four families and III (white collar) for two families in Study 1. In Study 2, the father's occupation was I/II for twenty-seven families, III (white collar) for four families, III (skilled manual) for nine families, and IV/V (semiskilled or unskilled for three families. Of the six families in Study 3, three were I/II, two were III (white collar), and one was III (skilled manual). The mean age difference between the siblings was 24 months (range 16–42 months) in Study 1, 26 months (range 12–57) in Study 2, and 27 months (range 18–40) in Study 3.

The observations were carried out in the home. Audiotape and paper-and-pencil recording methods were used, since videotaping was found to be too intrusive and to present problems for recording triadic interaction. To reduce the intrusive effect of the observer's presence, the observer paid at least one visit to the home before conducting the first observation; the same observer visited the family on each occasion. We emphasized to the mothers that we wished to study "normal" interaction between the siblings, both friendly and hostile, and to disrupt family patterns as little as possible. Mothers continued to carry out their usual domestic routines while we were present. The frequency of fights, arguments, and fantasy play during the observations suggests that our attempts to minimize intrusive effects were reasonably successful. Family conversation during the observation was tape-recorded and transcribed by the observer following the observation.

During the observations a running record was made in a lined notebook, with each line representing 10 seconds (see Dunn and Kendrick, 1982). A time marker was provided by an electronic bleeper. This running record included both precoded categories of behavior and narrative notes. Coding and categorization of the behavior was then performed at a number of different levels of detail for the different analyses reported and discussed in the book. For example, for the analysis of the disputes described in Chapters 2 and 3, the following aspects of behavior were categorized: (1) Emotional behavior, including categorization of intense negative and positive affect as part of the precoded items. (2) Categorization of acts such as "teasing" or "supporting" that involved inferences concerning the understanding of others' behavior; this required detailed narrative notes on the context of the behavior and the sequence of actions, in addition to the precoded items. (3) Coding of children's behavior in relation to transgression of social rules entailed categorization of topic of conflict and of children's response and communicative behavior; this required information from the narrative notes on the context and the verbal transcripts, in addition to the precoded items. For the details of such coding and categorization and the reliabilities, see Dunn and Munn (1985, 1986, 1987).

Appendix Table 1. Justifications in mother-child and sibling-child disputes, expressed as mean proportion of disputes with that partner (Study 2)

	Total justifications	Type of justification			
		Own feelings	Social rules	Material consequences	Others' feelings
Child					
18 months					
With mother	.04	.04	0	0	0
With sibling	.02	0	.01	0	0
24 months					
With mother	.11	.05	.01	0	.01
With sibling	.18	.04	.11	.01	.01
36 months					
With mother	.32	.15	.04	.05	0
With sibling	.28	.14	.06	.05	.01
Mother					
18 months	.33	.03	.09	.14	.04
24 months	.51	.04	.11	.27	.08
36 months	.55	.04	.15	.29	.04
Sibling					
18 months	.19	.07	.08	.05	.01
24 months	.39	.10	.18	.11	.01
36 months	.33	.10	.07	.17	.02

Child justifications: MANOVA shows significant overall effects of age (F [6, 158] = 10.04), of partner (F [3, 38] = 2.95). Univariate analyses show age effects significant for justifications by reference to own feelings, rules, material consequences (F [1, 80] = 13.95, 5.02, 18.45 respectively); justifications by reference to rules more frequent to sibling than to mother (F [1, 40] = 8.06).

Mother and sibling justifications: MANOVA shows significant overall effect of age (F [2, 77] = 18.05), of partner (F [1, 38] = 20.41). Univariate analyses show significant increase with age was in reference to material consequences (F [1, 80] = 16.14).

Appendix Table 2. Mean proportion of mother-child disputes focused on different topics, in which anger/distress, laughter, and justification were shown (Study 2)

	Child emotion		Mother justification	Child justification
Topic of dispute	Anger/ distress	Laugher		
18 months				
Rights	.24	.06	.48	–
Convention	.12	.06	.34	–
Destruction	.04	.10	.27	–
Aggression	–	.15	.34	–
24 months				
Rights	.13	.06	.54	–
Convention	.14	.03	.45	–
Destruction	.07	.12	.38	–
Aggression	.05	.14	.49	–
36 months				
Rights	.09	.04	.62	.35
Convention	.10	.07	.51	.32
Destruction	.07	.13	.49	.21
Aggression	–	.50	.35	.10

Log linear analyses show children more likely to show anger/distress in disputes over rights/conventions at 24 months; more likely to reason in disputes over rights at 36 months. Mothers were more likely to reason in disputes over rights at 18 months; over rights and conventions at 24 and 36 months. For details of these analyses see Dunn and Munn, 1987.

Appendix Table 3. Frequency of child appeals to mother following hostile acts by child and by sibling (Study 1)

Hostile acts	Appeal to mother	No appeal to mother
By child → sibling conflict (N = 125)	4	121
By sibling → sibling conflict (N = 99)	65	34

Difference tested with general linear model with binomial error and logistic link function. Mean deviance ratio = 8.706, p < .001.

Appendix Table 4. Children's responses to three topic categories of sibling-mother conflict (Study 2)

Children's response	(1) Aggression Mean proportion	SD	(2) Power Mean proportion	SD	(3) Rules Mean proportion	SD
Imitates sibling	.03[a]	.09	.21	.36	.27[a]	.29
Supports sibling	.19	.37	.04	.13	.05	.11
Supports mother	.00	.00	.07	.16	.05	.11
Punishes/prohibits sibling	.31[a,b]	.46	.02[b]	.09	.01[a]	.03
Laughs at mother/sibling (without other response)	.00[a]	.00	.04[c]	.19	.09[a,c]	.14
Watches	.31	.46	.26	.34	.36	.28
Ignores	.16	.35	.37[c]	.40	.17[c]	.20

a. Difference between category 1 and category 3 significant at p < .05.
b. Difference between category 1 and category 2 significant at p < .05.
c. Difference between category 2 and category 3 significant at p < .05.

Appendix Table 5. Children's responses to three affect categories of sibling-mother conflict (Study 2)

Children's response	(1) Sibling or mother intense negative Mean proportion	SD	(2) Sibling laughs Mean proportion	SD	(3) Neutral affect Mean proportion	SD
Imitates sibling	.14	.29	.34	.39	.25	.31
Supports sibling	.18	.34	.02	.07	.05	.17
Supports mother	.03	.90	.05	.22	.05	.10
Punishes/prohibits sibling	.01	.04	.00	.00	.02	.06
Laughs at mother/ sibling (without other response)	.03[a]	.10	.33[a,c]	.43	.04[c]	.09
Watches	.50	.37	.18	.37	.30	.33
Ignores	.12[b]	.25	.08[c]	.16	.30[b,c]	.30

a. Difference between category 1 and category 2 significant at p < .05.
b. Difference between category 1 and category 3 significant at p. < .05.
c. Difference between category 2 and category 3 significant at p. < .05.

Appendix 2

Narrative

See Chapter 7, p. 127:

The majority of the narratives included more than one clause and could be classified as narratives according to the definition of Labov and Waletzky (1967), as a sequence of two or more clauses that recapitulates experience in the same order as the original event. But the Umiker-Sebeok definition that included one-clause narratives was employed on the grounds that, when studying narrative in ongoing conversations, "it can be assumed that the listener will use the information gained through his familiarity with the context and co-text of the story to flesh out what he is being told happened. A simple utterance such as *John pushed him,* for example, while not a narrative if taken out of context, may be considered as such if one takes into account that the speaker and hearer are witness to a scene such as one boy crying and rubbing his head, while next to him stands a boy with a sheepish grin on his face. In such a situation, it is not necessary for the narrator to encode as part of his utterance that a fight resulted in an injury to one participant, or who sustained the injury and who caused it, and so forth" (Umiker-Sebeok, 1977, p. 92).

References

Arsenio, W. F., and Ford, M.E. 1985. The role of affective information in social-cognitive development: Children's differentiation of moral and conventional events. *Merrill-Palmer Quarterly, 31,* 1–17.

Bannister, D., and Agnew, J. 1977. The child's construing of self. In J. Cole, ed., *Nebraska symposium on motivation.* Lincoln: University of Nebraska Press.

Berenthal, B. I., and Fischer, K. W. 1978. Development of self-recognition in the infant. *Developmental Psychology, 14,* 44–50.

Bloom, L., and Capatides, J. B. 1987. Sources of meaning in the acquisition of complex syntax: The sample case of causality. *Journal of Experimental Child Psychology, 43,* 112–128.

Blum, L. 1980. *Friendship, altruism and morality.* London: Routledge.

——— 1987. Particularity and responsiveness. In J. Kagan, ed., *The emergence of morality in young children.* Chicago: University of Chicago Press.

Bower, G. 1981. Mood and memory. *American Psychologist, 36,* 129–148.

Bretherton, I. 1985. Attachment theory: Retrospect and prospect. In I. Bretherton and E. Waters, eds., Growing points of attachment theory and research. *Monographs of the Society for Research in Child Development, 50,* (1–2, no. 209).

——— McNew, S., and Beeghley-Smith, M. 1981. Early person knowledge as expressed in gestural and verbal communication: When do infants acquire a "theory of mind"? In M. E. Lamb and L. R. Sherrod, eds., *Infant social cognition.* Hillsdale, N.J.: Erlbaum.

Brice-Heath, S. 1983. *Ways with words: Language, life, and work in communities and classrooms.* Cambridge: Cambridge University Press.

Bridgeman, D. L. 1983. Benevolent babies: Emergence of the social self. In D. L. Bridgeman, ed., *The nature of prosocial development.* New York: Academic Press.

Bruner, J. S. 1977. Early social interaction and language acquisition. In H. R. Schaffer, ed., *Studies in mother-infant interaction*. London: Academic Press.

—— 1983. *Child's talk*. New York: Norton.

—— 1986. *Actual minds, possible worlds*. Cambridge, Mass.: Harvard University Press.

—— and Sherwood, V. 1976. Peekaboo and the learning of rule structures. In J. S. Bruner, A. Jolly, and K. Sylva, eds., *Play: Its role in development and evolution*. New York: Basic Books.

Burlingham, D., and Freud, A. 1944. *Infants without families*. London: Allen and Unwin.

Caillois, R. 1961. *Man, play and games*. New York: Free Press.

Carey, S. 1985. *Conceptual change in childhood*. Cambridge, Mass.: MIT Press.

Cosmides, L. 1985. Deduction or Darwinian algorithms? An explanation of the "elusive" content effect on the Wason Selection task. Diss., Department of Psychology and Social Relations, Harvard University.

—— and Tooby, J. 1987. From evolution to behavior: Evolutionary psychology as the missing link. In J. Dupré, ed., *The latest on the best: Essays on evolution and optimality*. Cambridge, Mass.: MIT Press.

Cummings, E. M. 1987. Coping with background anger. *Child Development, 58,* 976–984.

—— Zahn-Waxler, C., and Radke-Yarrow, M. 1981. Young children's responses to expressions of anger and affection by others in the family. *Child Development, 52,* 1274–1282.

—— Zahn-Waxler, C., and Radke-Yarrow, M. 1984. Developmental changes in children's reactions to anger in the home. *Journal of Child Psychology and Psychiatry, 25,* 63–74.

Dale, N. 1983. Early pretend play within the family. Diss., University of Cambridge.

Damon, W. 1977. *The social world of the child*. San Francisco: Jossey-Bass.

Darley, J. M., and Zanna, M. P. 1982. Making moral judgments. *American Scientist, 70,* 515–521.

Davison, A. 1966. Linguistic play and language acquisition. *Papers and reports on child language development*. Stanford, 1974.

Dinner, S. H. 1976. Social comparison and self-evaluation in children. Diss., Department of Psychology, Princeton University.

Douglas, M. 1966. *Purity and danger: An analysis of the concepts of taboo.* New York: Praeger.

Dunn, J., Bretherton, I., and Munn, P. 1987. Conversations about feeling states between mothers and their young children. *Developmental Psychology, 23,* 132–139.

—— and Dale, N. 1984. I a Daddy: 2-year-olds' collaboration in joint pretend with sibling and with mother. In I. Bretherton, ed., *Symbolic play: The development of social understanding.* New York: Academic Press.

—— and Kendrick, C. 1982. *Siblings: Love, envy, and understanding* Cambridge, Mass.: Harvard University Press.

—— and Munn, P. 1985. Becoming a family member: Family conflict and the development of social understanding. *Child Development, 56,* 480–492.

—— and Munn, P. 1986. Siblings and the development of prosocial behaviour. *International Journal of Behavioral Development, 9,* 265–284.

—— and Munn, P. 1987. Development of justification in disputes with mother and sibling. *Developmental Psychology, 23,* 791–798.

—— and Shatz, M. 1988. Becoming a conversationalist. Manuscript.

Edgeworth, M. and R. I. 1798. *Practical education.* London: Johnson.

Eisenberg, A. R., and Garvey, C. 1981. Children's use of verbal strategies in resolving conflicts. *Discourse Processes, 4,* 149–170.

Eisenberg-Berg, N., and Neal, C. 1979. Children's moral reasoning about their own spontaneous prosocial behavior. *Developmental Psychology, 15,* 228–229.

—— and Hand, M. 1979. The relationship of preschoolers' reasoning about prosocial moral conflicts to prosocial behavior. *Child Development, 50,* 356–363.

Ervin-Tripp, S. 1974. The comprehension and production of requests by children. *Papers and reports on child language development.* Stanford, 1974.

Fein, G. G. 1981. Pretend play in childhood: An integrative review. *Child Development, 52,* 1095–1118.

Feiring, C., Lewis, M., and Starr, M. D. 1984. Indirect effects and infants' reaction to strangers. *Developmental Psychology, 20,* 485–491.

Flavell, J. 1985. *Cognitive development,* 2nd ed. Englewood Cliffs, N.J.: Prentice-Hall.

Freud, S. 1966. *Introductory lectures on psychoanalysis.* New York: Norton.

Garvey, C. 1977. *Play.* Cambridge, Mass.: Harvard University Press.

Gelman, R., and Baillargeon, R. 1983. A review of some Piagetian concepts. In P. H. Mussen, ed., *Handbook of child psychology,* vol. 3, *Cognitive development.* New York: Wiley.

—— and Spelke, E. 1981. The development of thought about animate and inanimate: Implications for research on social cognition. In J. H. Flavell and L. Ross, eds., *Social cognitive development: Frontiers and possible futures.* Cambridge: Cambridge University Press.

Gilligan, C. 1982. *In a different voice: Psychological theory and women's development.* Cambridge, Mass.: Harvard University Press.

Goffman, E. 1971. *Interaction ritual.* Harmondsworth: Penguin Books.

Golinkoff, R., Harding, C. A., Carlson, V., and Sexton, M. E. 1984. The infant's perception of causal events: The distinction between animate and inanimate objects. In L. P. Lipsitt and C. Royce-Collier, eds., *Advances in infancy research,* vol. 3. Norwood, N.J.: Ablex.

Goodenough, F. L. 1931. *Anger in young children.* Minneapolis: University of Minnesota Press.

Guillame, P. 1926. *Imitation in children,* E. P. Halperin, trans. Chicago: University of Chicago Press.

Harkness, S., and Super, C. M. 1982. Why African children are so hard to test. In L. L. Adler, ed., *Cross-cultural research at issue.* New York: Academic Press.

—— Child-environment interactions in the socialization of affect. In M. Lewis and C. Saarni, eds., *The socialization of emotions.* New York: Plenum Press.

Hart, H. A. L. 1961. *The conception of law.* London: Oxford University Press.

Harter, S. 1983. Developmental perspectives on the self-system. In P. H. Mussen, ed., *Handbook of child psychology,* vol. 4, *Socialization, personality, and social development.* New York: Wiley.

Hay, D. F. 1979. Cooperative interactions and sharing between very young children and their parents. *Developmental Psychology, 15,* 647–653.

—— Murray, P., Cecire, S., and Nash, A. 1985. Social learning of social behavior in early life. *Child Development, 56,* 43–57.

—— Nash, A., and Pedersen, J. 1981. Responses of six-month-olds to the distress of their peers. *Child Development, 52,* 1071–1075.

Heckhausen, H. 1983. Concern with one's own competence: Developmental shifts in person-environment interaction. In D. Magnussen and V. Allen, eds., *Human development: An interactional perspective.* New York: Academic Press.

—— 1987. Acquiring the notion of competence in the second year. Developmental promotion in the context of the infant's joint action with the mother. Manuscript.

Hoffman, M. L. 1976. Empathy, role-taking, guilt, and development of altruistic motives. In T. Likona, ed. *Moral development: Current theory and research.* New York: Holt, Rinehart and Winston.

—— 1981. Perspectives on the difference between understanding people and understanding others: The role of affect. In J. H. Flavell and L. Ross, eds., *Social cognitive development: Frontiers and possible futures.* Cambridge: Cambridge University Press.

Hood, L., and Bloom, L. 1979. What, when, and how about why: A longitudinal study of early expressions of causality. *Monographs of the Society for Research in Child Development, 44* (6, no. 181).

Isaacs, S. 1937. *Social development in young children: A study of beginnings.* New York: Harcourt, Brace.

Izard, C. E. 1978. On the ontogenesis of emotions and emotion-cognition relationships in infancy. In M. Lewis and L. A. Rosenblum, eds., *The development of affect.* New York: Plenum Press.

James, W. 1890. *The principles of psychology.* New York: Holt.

Johnson, C. N., and Wellman, H. M. 1980. Children's developing understanding of mental verbs: Remember, know and guess. *Child Development, 51,* 1095–1102.

—— 1982. Children's developing conceptions of the mind and brain. *Child Development, 53,* 222–234.

Justin, F. 1932. A genetic study of laughter provoking stimuli. *Child Development, 3,* 114–135.

Kagan, J. 1981. *The second year.* Cambridge, Mass.: Harvard University Press.

—— 1984. *The nature of the child.* New York: Basic Books.

Kaye, K. 1982. *The mental and social life of babies.* London: Methuen.

Klinnert, M. D., Campos, J. J., Sorce, J. F., Emde, R. N., and Svejda, M. 1983. Emotions as behavior regulators: Social referencing in infancy. In R. Plutchik and H. Kellerman, eds., *Emotion: Theory, research, and experience,* vol. 2. New York: Academic Press.

Kohlberg, L. 1976. Moral stages and moralization: The cognitive-developmental. In T. Lickona, ed., *Moral development and behavior: Theory, research, and social issues.* New York: Holt, Rinehart and Winston.

Krebs, D. 1983. Commentary and critique: Psychological and philosophical approaches to prosocial development. In D. L. Bridgeman, ed., *The nature of prosocial development.* New York: Academic Press.

Labov, W., and Waletzky, J. 1967. Narrative analysis: Oral versions of personal experience. In J. Helm, ed., *Essays in the verbal and visual arts.* Seattle: American Ethnological Society.

Lewin, K. 1942. Changes in social sensitivity in child and adult. *Childhood Education, 19* 53–57.

Lewis, M., and Brooks-Gunn, J. 1979. *Social cognition and the acquisition of self.* New York: Plenum Press.

Lytton, H. 1977. Correlates of compliance and the rudiments of conscience in two-year-old boys. *Canadian Journal of Behavioral Science, 9,* 243–251.

———— 1979. Disciplinary encounters between young boys and their mothers: Is there a contingency system? *Developmental Psychology, 15,* 256–268.

Maccoby, E. M., and Martin, J. A. 1983. Socialization in the context of the family: Parent-child interaction. In P. H. Mussen, ed., *Handbook of child psychology,* vol. 4, *Socialization, personality, and social development.*

Malatesta, C. Z., and Izard, C. E. 1982. The ontogenesis of human social signals: From biological imperative to symbol utilization. In N. Fox and R. J. Davidson, eds., *Affective development: A psychological perspective.* Hillsdale, N.J.: Erlbaum.

Mahler, M. S., Pine, F., and Bergman, A. 1975. *The psychological birth of the human infant.* New York: Basic Books.

Markman, E. M. 1981 Two different principles of conceptual organization. In M. E. Lamb and A. L. Brown, eds., *Advances in developmental psychology,* vol. 1. Hillsdale, N.J.: Erlbaum.

Masters, J. E. 1971. Social comparison by young children. *Young Children, 3,* 37–60.

McKain, K., Stern, D. N., Goldberg, A., and Moeller, B. 1985. The identification of correspondence between an infant's internal affective state and the facial display of that affect by another. Manuscript.

Mead, G. H. 1934. *Mind, self, and society.* Chicago: University of Chicago Press.

Millar, S. 1968. *The psychology of play.* Harmondsworth: Penguin Books.

Miller, P., and Garvey, C. 1984. Mother-baby role play: Its origins in social support. In I. Bretherton, ed., *Symbolic play: The development of social understanding.* New York: Academic Press.

——— and Sperry, L. L. 1987. The socialization of anger and aggression. *Merrill Palmer Quarterly, 33,* 1–32.

Minton, C., Kagan, J., and Levine, J. A. 1971. Maternal control and obedience in the two year old. *Child Development, 42,* 2873–2894.

Much, N. C., and Shweder, R. 1978. Speaking of rules: The analysis of culture in breach. In W. Damon, ed., *Moral development: New directions for child development.* San Francisco: Jossey-Bass.

Murphy, L. B. 1937. *Social behavior and child personality.* New York: Columbia University Press.

Nelson, J. 1753. *Essay on the government of children under three heads, viz, health, manners and education.* London: Dodsley.

Nelson, Katherine. 1981. Social cognition in a script framework. In J. H. Flavell and L. Ross, eds., *Social cognitive development: Frontiers and possible futures.* Cambridge: Cambridge University Press.

Nezworski, T., Stein, N. L., and Trabasso, T. 1981. Story structure versus context in children's recall. *Journal of Memory and Language, 21,* 196–201.

Nicholich, L. A. 1975. A longitudinal study of representation play in relation to spontaneous initiation and the development of multiword utterances. Government Report, N.I.E. no. NE-6-11-3-0021.

Ochs, E. 1987. *Culture and language acquisition: Acquiring communicative competence in a Samoan village.* Cambridge: Cambridge University Press.

Packer, M. J. 1986. Social interaction as practical activity: Implications for social and moral development. Proceedings of conference on social process and social development. Miami, Fla., January 1986.

Parpal, M., and Maccoby, E. E. 1985. Maternal responsiveness and subsequent child compliance. *Child Development, 56,* 1326–1334.

Perner, J., Leekham, S. R., and Wimmer, H. 1987. Three-year-olds' difficulty with false belief. *British Journal of Developmental Psychology, 5,* 125–137.

Piaget, J. 1932. *The moral judgment of the child.* New York: Free Press, 1965.

Radke-Yarrow, M., Zahn-Waxler, C., and Chapman, M. 1983. Children's prosocial dispositions and behavior. In P. H. Mussen, ed., *Handbook of child psychology,* vol. 4, *Socialization, personality, and social development.* New York: Wiley.

Rest, J. R. 1983. Morality. In P. H. Mussen, ed., *Handbook of child psychology,* vol. 3, *Cognitive development.* New York: Wiley.

Rheingold, H. L., and Hay, D. F. 1978. Prosocial behavior of the very young. In G. S. Stent, ed., *Morality as a biological phenomenon.* Berlin: Dahlem Konferenzen.

—— Hay, D. F., and West, M. J. 1976. Sharing in the second year of life. *Child Development, 47,* 1148–1158.

Ross, H. S. 1982. Establishment of social games among toddlers, *Developmental Psychology, 18,* 509–518.

—— Goldman, B. D., and Hay, D. F. 1979. Features and functions of infant games. In B. Sutton-Smith, ed., *Play and learning.* New York: Gardner Press.

Ruble, D. N., Boggiano, A. K., Feldman, N. S., and Loebl, J. H. 1980. Developmental analysis of the role of social comparison in self-evaluation. *Developmental Psychology, 16,* 105–115.

—— Feldman, N. S., and Boggiano, A. K. 1976. Social comparison between young children in achievement situations. *Developmental Psychology, 12,* 192–197.

Sagi, A., and Hoffman, M. L. 1976. Empathic distress in the newborn. *Developmental Psychology, 12,* 175–176.

Sampson, A. and S. 1985. *Oxford book of ages.* London: Oxford University Press.

Saussure, A. de. 1828–1832. *L'education progressive, ou etudes du cours de la vie.* Trans. London: Longmans, 1839.

Scaife, M., and Bruner, J. S. 1955. The capacity for joint visual attention in the infant. *Nature, 253,* 265–266.

Schaffer, H. R., and Crook, C. K. 1979. Child compliance and maternal control techniques. *Developmental Psychology, 16,* 54–61.

Schulz, T. R. 1980. Development of the concept of intention. In A. Collins, ed., *Minnesota symposium on child psychology, 13.* Hillsdale, N.J.: Erlbaum.

———— 1976. A cognitive-developmental analysis of humour. In A. J. Chapman and H. C. Foot, eds., *Humour and laughter: Theory, research and applications.* London: Wiley.

Seligman, M. E. P., and Peterson, C. 1986. A learned helplessness perspective on childhood depression: Theory and research. In M. Rutter, C. E. Izard, and P. B. Read, eds., *Depression in young people: Clinical and developmental perspectives.* New York: Guilford Press.

Selman, R. L. 1980. *The growth of interpersonal understanding.* New York: Academic Press.

Shantz, C. U. 1983. Social cognition. In P. H. Mussen, ed., *Handbook of Child Psychology,* vol. 3, *Cognitive development.* New York: Wiley.

Shatz, M., Wellman, H. M., and Silber, S. 1983. The acquisition of mental verbs: A systematic investigation of the first reference to mental state. *Cognition, 14,* 301–322.

Shweder, R. A., Mahapatra, M., and Miller, J. G. 1987. Culture and moral development. In J. Kagan, ed., *The emergence of moral concepts in young children.* Chicago: University of Chicago Press.

———— and Much, N. C. 1986. Determinants of meaning: Discourse and moral socialization. Manuscript.

———— Turiel, E., and Much, N. C. 1981. The moral intuitions of the child. In J. H. Flavell and L. Ross, eds., *Social cognitive development: Frontiers and possible futures.* Cambridge: Cambridge University Press.

Simner, M. L. 1971. Newborn's response to the cry of another infant. *Developmental Psychology, 5,* 135–150.

Singer, M. G. 1963. *Generalisation in ethics.* London: Eyre and Spottiswoode.

Spelke, E. S., and Cortelyou, A. 1981. Perceptual aspects of social knowing: Looking and listening in infancy. In M. E. Lamb and L. R. Sherrod, eds., *Infant social cognition.* Hillsdale, N.J.: Erlbaum.

Spitz, R. A. 1957. *No and yes: On the genesis of human communi-cation.* New York: International Universities Press.

Sroufe, L. A. 1979. Socioemotional development. In J. D. Osofsky, ed., *Handbook of infant development.* New York: Wiley.

———— and Wunsch, J. 1972. The development of laughter in the first year of life. *Child Development, 43,* 1326–1344.

Stanjek, K. 1978. Das Uberreichen von Gaben: Funktion und En-twicklung in den ersten Lebensjahren. *Zeitschrift fur Entwicks-lungspsychologie und Pedagogische Psychologie, 10,* 103–113.

Stern, D. N. 1977. *The first relationship.* Cambridge, Mass.: Harvard University Press.

———— 1985. *The interpersonal world of the child.* New York: Basic Books.

Stern, W. 1924. *Psychology of early childhood.* New York: Holt.

Strayer, F. F., Wareing, S., and Rushton, J. P. 1979. Social constraints on naturally occurring preschool altruism. *Ethology and Socio-biology, 1,* 3–11.

Sullivan, H. S. 1940. *Conceptions of modern psychiatry.* London: Tavistock Press.

———— 1953. *The interpersonal theory of psychiatry.* New York: Norton.

Sully, J. 1896. *Studies of childhood.* New York: Appleton.

Tizard, B., and Hughes, M. 1984. *Young children learning.* London: Fontana.

Trevarthen, C. 1977. Descriptive analyses of infant communicative behavior. In H. R. Schaffer, ed., *Studies in mother-infant inter-action.* London: Academic Press.

———— and Hubley, P. 1978. Secondary intersubjectivity: Confidence, confiders and acts of meaning in the first year. In A. Lock, ed., *Action, gesture and symbol.* New York: Academic Press.

Umiker-Sebeok, D. J. 1977. Preschool children's intraconversational narratives. *Journal of Child Language, 6,* 91–109.

Vaughn, B. E., Kopp, C. B., and Krakow, J. B. 1984. The emergence and consolidation of self-control from eighteen to thirty months of age: Normative trends and individual differences. *Child De-velopment, 55,* 990–1004.

Watson-Gegeo, K. A., and Gegeo, D. 1987. The social world of Kwara'ae children: Acquisition of language and values. Manu-script.

Wellman, H. M. 1985. The origins of metacognition. In D. For-rest-Pressley, G. MacKinnon, and T. Waller, eds., *Metacognition, cognition, and human performance*. New York: Academic Press.

——— 1986. First steps in the child's theorizing about the mind. Manuscript.

——— and Estes, D. 1986. Early understanding of mental entities: A reexamination of childhood realism. *Child Development, 57,* 910–923.

Wimmer, H., and Perner, J. 1983. Beliefs about beliefs: Representation and constraining function of wrong beliefs in young children's understanding of deception. *Cognition, 13,* 103–128.

Wolf, D. 1982. Understanding others: A longitudinal case study of the concept of independent agency. In G. E. Forman, ed., *Action and thought*. New York: Academic Press.

——— Rygh, J., and Altshuler, J. 1984. Agency and experience: Actions and states in play narratives. In I. Bretherton, ed., *Symbolic play: The development of social understanding*. New York: Academic Press.

Yarrow, M. R., and Waxler, C. Z. 1976. Dimensions and correlates of prosocial behavior in young children. *Child Development, 47,* 118–125.

Youniss, J. 1980. *Parents and peers in social development: A Sullivan-Piaget perspective*. Chicago: University of Chicago Press.

Zahn-Waxler, C., and Radke-Yarrow, M. 1982. The development of altruism: Alternative research strategies. In N. Eisenberg-Berg, ed., *The development of prosocial behavior*. New York: Academic Press.

Index